365 Days of Affirmations for Divine Abundance
By Lisa Glanzel

First Edition: January 2016
Published by: Lisa Glanzel and Earth And Beyond Crystal Therapies, LLC

.

Edited by: Courtney Lindemann – CourtneyEdits.com
Cover Design by: Tammy Burkle – Studio631.com
Cover Photo: ShutterStock Image ID: 280723916 – RugliG

ISBN:-10: 1511985038
ISBN-13: 978-1511985031

"Simple yet Powerful Practice! This book is the key to unlocking true Divine Abundance in your life. Thank you Lisa for this incredible tool. I look forward to sharing this with my clients and to use it everyday!"

~ Flora Sage, www.FloraSage.com

"365 Days of Affirmation for Divine Abundance is essential for anyone wanting to really align with all the possibilities of abundance. This book elegantly and efficiently navigates you daily in not only affirming your right to abundance, but also assists you in being open to receiving it in every way! Thank you Lisa, this book is amazing!!!"

~ Shakti Wallace – One Ascension International™

"BAM! This book rocks! I LOVE this book. The way Lisa has set it up, I retain the affirmation throughout the day. Repeating and writing key words throughout the day really allows the thought behind it to sink in. It tucks into your bag easily, which allows you to be able to write your thoughts throughout the day. Thank you for an easy affirmation "workbook," Lisa! I highly recommend this to everyone who strives to improve their day and life."

~ Denise Neal www.deniseneal.com

"There is nothing more powerful than the written word. I look forward to using this book as an inspiring tool each and every day, this is truly an uplifting book and reminder of the true abundance in my life, Thank you Lisa!"

~ Tammy Burkle www.studio631.com

Dedication

This book is dedicated to all the people who have touched my life, taught me about myself, encouraged me to follow my dreams and to move beyond limiting beliefs.

Acknowledgements

I am extremely grateful for my friends, family, teachers, coaches, and mentors. Each one plays a different role and touches my life in so many ways. I am honored to have each of you in my life.

There are no accidents. I believe each of you came into my life at the perfect time and encouraged me to be the very best I can be. It has not always been easy. Growth never is. We all have unique gifts and a unique journey. I am grateful to be writing these words and to be able to share this workbook for all to reflect on. My wish is for the presence of divine abundance in each of your lives.

Thank you! Thank you! Thank you!

Daily Divine Abundance Statement

Divine abundance is all around me.

Through the grace of divine love, I live each day in gratitude.

I am blessed.

I am loved.

I deserve the best life has to offer.

Thank you! Thank you! Thank you!

Introduction

I believe that divine abundance is possible even if we are not consciously aware. When we make the decision to recognize the signs and symbols that are presented to us, we begin to see that the Universe always responds with like energy. I am of the mindset that when we approach each day with optimism, we can impact our reality. Does this mean that we will never experience hardship or challenges in our life? No!!! Life happens. However, when we consistently work on ourselves to change our energy patterns and to raise our vibrations, we begin to recognize issues and blocks that may be holding us back. The more we do the work and show up for ourselves, the greater the impact we have on our energetic patterns, and the easier it becomes to begin the process of healing and to release the patterns caused by limiting beliefs.

To introduce myself, I am Lisa, seeker of universal knowledge and student of the Universe. I have a true desire to share what I have learned in my life and in my practice— to guide others to recognize the infinite possibilities that are available.

I am so excited that you have been guided to pick up my book: 365 Days of Affirmations for Divine Abundance. This book was written from my heart and with divine guidance. 365 Days of Affirmations for Divine Abundance is a reminder to myself and to everyone guided to work with this book, that divine abundance is always present in all that we do.

I realize that not everyone may have the same beliefs, however, if this book has found you, more than likely, we are of like minds. Through this process, I urge you to dig deep and allow great things to manifest for you.

Be authentic!

Show up!

Stay true!

Do the work!

Let go!

Believe amazing results are possible!

Manifest a new reality!

Recommendations for use

As you go through this book, keep an open mind. You may not resonate with each affirmation. If you do not – that is perfect. Substitute what feels right for you. My words and guidance are just that: guidance for you to step into your magnificence.

If you choose to follow the book as it is laid out, each day presents a new affirmation and the opportunity to anchor yourself in that affirmation and to set your intentions for the day.

There are four parts to each day. I like to start my day with the affirmation and setting my intentions. If you resonate to a different time during the day, choose the time that feels right for you.

The four action items are...

1. The affirmation.

2. The opportunity to write the affirmation a few times to anchor in the words. Feel free to insert your own words, if so guided.

3. Write key words to reflect on during the day. This practice helps to keep your energies positive.

4. Declare your love for yourself by allowing yourself to express the words "I love you ____" each day. Allow the words to flow and do not censor yourself. If this is difficult at first, be kind and gentle. With practice, it becomes easier.

Most of all, have fun and enjoy the process!

DAY 1

Divine abundance is my natural state of being
and I am grateful for my many blessings.

♡ ♡ ♡ ♡ ♡

Set your intentions for the day by...

Repeating the affirmation

_____

_____

_____

Thinking and writing positive thoughts

_____

_____

_____

Loving yourself

_____

_____

_____

DAY 2

I am grateful for my successes and the presence
of divine abundance in my life.

♡ ♡ ♡ ♡ ♡

Set your intentions for the day by...

Repeating the affirmation

_____

_____

_____

Thinking and writing positive thoughts

_____

_____

_____

Loving yourself

_____

_____

_____

DAY 3

I affirm that divine abundance is all around
me and I am grateful for the state of grace.

♡　♡　♡　♡　♡

Set your intentions for the day by...

Repeating the affirmation

_____

_____

_____

Thinking and writing positive thoughts

_____

_____

_____

Loving yourself

_____

_____

_____

DAY 4

I am a magnet for divine abundance and I am grateful for the prosperity and success that it brings to me.

♡　♡　♡　♡　♡

Set your intentions for the day by...

Repeating the affirmation

_____

_____

_____

Thinking and writing positive thoughts

_____

_____

_____

Loving yourself

_____

_____

_____

DAY 5

I am grateful for divine abundance,
success, and prosperity in my life.

♡ ♡ ♡ ♡ ♡

Set your intentions for the day by...

Repeating the affirmation

_____

_____

_____

Thinking and writing positive thoughts

_____

_____

_____

Loving yourself

_____

_____

_____

DAY 6

Divine abundance flows easily and effortlessly into my life.
I am grateful to live in the flow of this blessing.

♡ ♡ ♡ ♡ ♡

Set your intentions for the day by...

Repeating the affirmation

_____

_____

_____

Thinking and writing positive thoughts

_____

_____

_____

Loving yourself

_____

_____

_____

DAY 7

I am grateful and blessed that miracles are a part of my
daily life and I live in divine abundance.

♡　♡　♡　♡　♡

Set your intentions for the day by...

Repeating the affirmation

_____

_____

_____

Thinking and writing positive thoughts

_____

_____

_____

Loving yourself

_____

_____

_____

DAY 8

I am blessed. Divine abundance is easy.
I am grateful for all that it brings.

♡   ♡   ♡   ♡   ♡

Set your intentions for the day by...

Repeating the affirmation

_____

_____

_____

Thinking and writing positive thoughts

_____

_____

_____

Loving yourself

_____

_____

_____

DAY 9

I am grateful that I experience divine
abundance in all areas of my life.

♡ ♡ ♡ ♡ ♡

Set your intentions for the day by...

Repeating the affirmation

_____

_____

_____

Thinking and writing positive thoughts

_____

_____

_____

Loving yourself

_____

_____

_____

DAY 10

Divine abundance is all around me
and I am grateful.

♡ ♡ ♡ ♡ ♡

Set your intentions for the day by...

Repeating the affirmation

_____

_____

_____

Thinking and writing positive thoughts

_____

_____

_____

Loving yourself

_____

_____

_____

DAY 11

I am grateful that I am blessed
with divine abundance.

♡　♡　♡　♡　♡

Set your intentions for the day by...

Repeating the affirmation

_____

_____

_____

Thinking and writing positive thoughts

_____

_____

_____

Loving yourself

_____

_____

_____

DAY 12

Divine abundance is reflected in everything I do.
I am grateful for the blessings I receive.

♡ ♡ ♡ ♡ ♡

Set your intentions for the day by...

Repeating the affirmation

_____

_____

_____

Thinking and writing positive thoughts

_____

_____

_____

Loving yourself

_____

_____

_____

DAY 13

Success, prosperity, and divine abundance are all around me. I am grateful for the opportunities that they bring.

♡ ♡ ♡ ♡ ♡

Set your intentions for the day by...

Repeating the affirmation

_____

_____

_____

Thinking and writing positive thoughts

_____

_____

_____

Loving yourself

_____

_____

_____

DAY 14

I am grateful for the gift of divine
abundance in my life.

♡　♡　♡　♡　♡

Set your intentions for the day by...

Repeating the affirmation

_____

_____

_____

Thinking and writing positive thoughts

_____

_____

_____

Loving yourself

_____

_____

_____

DAY 15

Divine abundance can be seen in the everyday activities in my life. I am grateful to recognize this blessing.

♡　♡　♡　♡　♡

Set your intentions for the day by...

Repeating the affirmation

_____

_____

_____

Thinking and writing positive thoughts

_____

_____

_____

Loving yourself

_____

_____

_____

DAY 16

Divine abundance and miracles are a part of
my everyday life and I am grateful.

♡   ♡   ♡   ♡   ♡

Set your intentions for the day by...

Repeating the affirmation

_____

_____

_____

Thinking and writing positive thoughts

_____

_____

_____

Loving yourself

_____

_____

_____

DAY 17

My heart is open and grateful to receive
divine abundance in my life.

♡ ♡ ♡ ♡ ♡

Set your intentions for the day by...

Repeating the affirmation

_____

_____

_____

Thinking and writing positive thoughts

_____

_____

_____

Loving yourself

_____

_____

_____

DAY 18

I attract divine abundance easily and effortlessly.
I am open and grateful for what it brings.

♡ ♡ ♡ ♡ ♡

Set your intentions for the day by...

Repeating the affirmation

_____

_____

_____

Thinking and writing positive thoughts

_____

_____

_____

Loving yourself

_____

_____

_____

DAY 19

I am grateful to recognize the flow
of divine abundance in my life.

♡　♡　♡　♡　♡

Set your intentions for the day by...

Repeating the affirmation

_____

_____

_____

Thinking and writing positive thoughts

_____

_____

_____

Loving yourself

_____

_____

_____

DAY 20

Divine abundance blesses my life every
moment of my day and I am grateful.

♡ ♡ ♡ ♡ ♡

Set your intentions for the day by...

Repeating the affirmation

_____

_____

_____

Thinking and writing positive thoughts

_____

_____

_____

Loving yourself

_____

_____

_____

DAY 21

I am grateful and love that I am blessed with divine abundance in all parts of my life.

♡ ♡ ♡ ♡ ♡

Set your intentions for the day by...

Repeating the affirmation

_____

_____

_____

Thinking and writing positive thoughts

_____

_____

_____

Loving yourself

_____

_____

_____

DAY 22

Thank you for divine abundance.
I am grateful for my life.

♡   ♡   ♡   ♡   ♡

Set your intentions for the day by...

Repeating the affirmation

_____

_____

_____

Thinking and writing positive thoughts

_____

_____

_____

Loving yourself

_____

_____

_____

DAY 23

The more I am grateful for divine abundance in my life,
the more divine abundance I receive.

♡ ♡ ♡ ♡ ♡

Set your intentions for the day by...

Repeating the affirmation

_____

_____

_____

Thinking and writing positive thoughts

_____

_____

_____

Loving yourself

_____

_____

_____

DAY 24

I am in constant flow for divine abundance and
I am grateful for all it brings to my life.

♡ ♡ ♡ ♡ ♡

Set your intentions for the day by...

Repeating the affirmation

_____

_____

_____

Thinking and writing positive thoughts

_____

_____

_____

Loving yourself

_____

_____

_____

DAY 25

Gratitude opens the door for divine
abundance in my life.

♡ ♡ ♡ ♡ ♡

Set your intentions for the day by...

Repeating the affirmation

_____

_____

_____

Thinking and writing positive thoughts

_____

_____

_____

Loving yourself

_____

_____

_____

DAY 26

I am grateful that I recognize divine
abundance in everything I do.

♡ ♡ ♡ ♡ ♡

Set your intentions for the day by...

Repeating the affirmation

_____

_____

_____

Thinking and writing positive thoughts

_____

_____

_____

Loving yourself

_____

_____

_____

DAY 27

Divine abundance consistently manifests
in my life and I am grateful.

$\heartsuit \quad \heartsuit \quad \heartsuit \quad \heartsuit \quad \heartsuit$

Set your intentions for the day by...

Repeating the affirmation

_____

_____

_____

Thinking and writing positive thoughts

_____

_____

_____

Loving yourself

_____

_____

_____

DAY 28

I am grateful that divine abundance
is always available to me.

♡ ♡ ♡ ♡ ♡

Set your intentions for the day by...

Repeating the affirmation

_____

_____

_____

Thinking and writing positive thoughts

_____

_____

_____

Loving yourself

_____

_____

_____

DAY 29

Divine abundance is present in my life.
I am grateful for all I receive.

♡　♡　♡　♡　♡

Set your intentions for the day by...

Repeating the affirmation

_____

_____

_____

Thinking and writing positive thoughts

_____

_____

_____

Loving yourself

_____

_____

_____

DAY 30

I am open to receive divine abundance
and gratefully accept it into my life.

♡　♡　♡　♡　♡

Set your intentions for the day by...

Repeating the affirmation

_____

_____

_____

Thinking and writing positive thoughts

_____

_____

_____

Loving yourself

_____

_____

_____

DAY 31

The more grateful I am, the more
divine abundance is available to me.

♡　♡　♡　♡　♡

Set your intentions for the day by...

Repeating the affirmation

_____

_____

_____

Thinking and writing positive thoughts

_____

_____

_____

Loving yourself

_____

_____

_____

DAY 32

Divine abundance and gratitude
are significant in my life.

♡ ♡ ♡ ♡ ♡

Set your intentions for the day by...

Repeating the affirmation

_____

_____

_____

Thinking and writing positive thoughts

_____

_____

_____

Loving yourself

_____

_____

_____

DAY 33

I am grateful for divine abundance.

♡　♡　♡　♡　♡

Set your intentions for the day by...

Repeating the affirmation

_____

_____

_____

Thinking and writing positive thoughts

_____

_____

_____

Loving yourself

_____

_____

_____

DAY 34

Divine abundance is present in all areas of my life.
I am grateful for the miracles that it brings.

♡ ♡ ♡ ♡ ♡

Set your intentions for the day by...

Repeating the affirmation

_____

_____

_____

Thinking and writing positive thoughts

_____

_____

_____

Loving yourself

_____

_____

_____

DAY 35

I am grateful that divine abundance
is part of my daily life.

♡　♡　♡　♡　♡

Set your intentions for the day by...

Repeating the affirmation

_____

_____

_____

Thinking and writing positive thoughts

_____

_____

_____

Loving yourself

_____

_____

_____

DAY 36

Divine abundance is a natural part of my life.
I am grateful for the many blessings that have manifested.

♡ ♡ ♡ ♡ ♡

Set your intentions for the day by...

Repeating the affirmation

_____

_____

_____

Thinking and writing positive thoughts

_____

_____

_____

Loving yourself

_____

_____

_____

DAY 37

Gratitude and divine abundance are
connected to all areas of my life.

♡   ♡   ♡   ♡   ♡

Set your intentions for the day by...

Repeating the affirmation

_____

_____

_____

Thinking and writing positive thoughts

_____

_____

_____

Loving yourself

_____

_____

_____

DAY 38

I am grateful that I am blessed with the opportunities that divine abundance provides me.

♡ ♡ ♡ ♡ ♡

Set your intentions for the day by...

Repeating the affirmation

_____

_____

_____

Thinking and writing positive thoughts

_____

_____

_____

Loving yourself

_____

_____

_____

DAY 39

I accept divine abundance into my
life with gratitude and love.

♡　♡　♡　♡　♡

Set your intentions for the day by...

Repeating the affirmation

_____

_____

_____

Thinking and writing positive thoughts

_____

_____

_____

Loving yourself

_____

_____

_____

DAY 40

I am blessed and grateful for divine
abundance in my life.

♡ ♡ ♡ ♡ ♡

Set your intentions for the day by...

Repeating the affirmation

_____

_____

_____

Thinking and writing positive thoughts

_____

_____

_____

Loving yourself

_____

_____

_____

DAY 41

I am grateful that I am successful,
prosperous, and gifted with divine abundance.

♡ ♡ ♡ ♡ ♡

Set your intentions for the day by...

Repeating the affirmation

_____

_____

_____

Thinking and writing positive thoughts

_____

_____

_____

Loving yourself

_____

_____

_____

DAY 42

I am always open to the flow of divine abundance.
I gratefully accept the beautiful gifts into my life.

♡　♡　♡　♡　♡

Set your intentions for the day by...

Repeating the affirmation

_____

_____

_____

Thinking and writing positive thoughts

_____

_____

_____

Loving yourself

_____

_____

_____

DAY 43

I am grateful for divine abundance and
blessed with the miracles it brings into my life.

♡　♡　♡　♡　♡

Set your intentions for the day by...

Repeating the affirmation

_____

_____

_____

Thinking and writing positive thoughts

_____

_____

_____

Loving yourself

_____

_____

_____

DAY 44

I trust that divine abundance is always present
and I am grateful for all that it brings.

♡ ♡ ♡ ♡ ♡

Set your intentions for the day by...

Repeating the affirmation

_____

_____

_____

Thinking and writing positive thoughts

_____

_____

_____

Loving yourself

_____

_____

_____

DAY 45

Divine abundance is a miracle in my life
and I am eternally grateful.

$\heartsuit$ $\heartsuit$ $\heartsuit$ $\heartsuit$ $\heartsuit$

Set your intentions for the day by...

Repeating the affirmation

_____

_____

_____

Thinking and writing positive thoughts

_____

_____

_____

Loving yourself

_____

_____

_____

DAY 46

I am grateful that I can easily see how
divine abundance is part of my life.

♡ ♡ ♡ ♡ ♡

Set your intentions for the day by...

Repeating the affirmation

_____

_____

_____

Thinking and writing positive thoughts

_____

_____

_____

Loving yourself

_____

_____

_____

DAY 47

Divine abundance is always available to me no matter what is going on in my life. I am grateful.

♡   ♡   ♡   ♡   ♡

Set your intentions for the day by...

Repeating the affirmation

_____

_____

_____

Thinking and writing positive thoughts

_____

_____

_____

Loving yourself

_____

_____

_____

DAY 48

I see divine abundance in everything I do
and I am grateful for this sight.

♡ ♡ ♡ ♡ ♡

Set your intentions for the day by...

Repeating the affirmation

_____

_____

_____

Thinking and writing positive thoughts

_____

_____

_____

Loving yourself

_____

_____

_____

DAY 49

Divine abundance and gratitude are
key components of my life.

♡　♡　♡　♡　♡

Set your intentions for the day by...

Repeating the affirmation

_____

_____

_____

Thinking and writing positive thoughts

_____

_____

_____

Loving yourself

_____

_____

_____

DAY 50

I know that I am blessed. Divine abundance
is all around me and I am grateful.

♡ ♡ ♡ ♡ ♡

Set your intentions for the day by...

Repeating the affirmation

_____

_____

_____

Thinking and writing positive thoughts

_____

_____

_____

Loving yourself

_____

_____

_____

DAY 51

Where there is gratitude, there is divine abundance.

♡ ♡ ♡ ♡ ♡

Set your intentions for the day by...

Repeating the affirmation

_____

_____

_____

Thinking and writing positive thoughts

_____

_____

_____

Loving yourself

_____

_____

_____

DAY 52

My heart is open and I give thanks for the divine abundance in my life. I am grateful for all that I receive.

♡ ♡ ♡ ♡ ♡

Set your intentions for the day by...

Repeating the affirmation

_____

_____

_____

Thinking and writing positive thoughts

_____

_____

_____

Loving yourself

_____

_____

_____

DAY 53

The universe showers me with divine
abundance and gratitude creates more.

♡ ♡ ♡ ♡ ♡

Set your intentions for the day by...

Repeating the affirmation

_____

_____

_____

Thinking and writing positive thoughts

_____

_____

_____

Loving yourself

_____

_____

_____

DAY 54

Divine abundance flows easily to me and
I am grateful for my many blessings.

♡　♡　♡　♡　♡

Set your intentions for the day by...

Repeating the affirmation

_____

_____

_____

Thinking and writing positive thoughts

_____

_____

_____

Loving yourself

_____

_____

_____

DAY 55

I am grateful that divine abundance is
part of everything I do.

♡   ♡   ♡   ♡   ♡

Set your intentions for the day by...

Repeating the affirmation

_____

_____

_____

Thinking and writing positive thoughts

_____

_____

_____

Loving yourself

_____

_____

_____

DAY 56

I easily manifest divine abundance in my life
through gratitude for all that I have.

♡ ♡ ♡ ♡ ♡

Set your intentions for the day by...

Repeating the affirmation

_____

_____

_____

Thinking and writing positive thoughts

_____

_____

_____

Loving yourself

_____

_____

_____

DAY 57

Divine abundance is in constant flow in my life.
I am grateful for how easy and effortless life is.

♡ ♡ ♡ ♡ ♡

Set your intentions for the day by...

Repeating the affirmation

_____

_____

_____

Thinking and writing positive thoughts

_____

_____

_____

Loving yourself

_____

_____

_____

DAY 58

I am grateful for increased wealth, prosperity, success, and divine abundance in my life.

♡　♡　♡　♡　♡

Set your intentions for the day by...

Repeating the affirmation

_____

_____

_____

Thinking and writing positive thoughts

_____

_____

_____

Loving yourself

_____

_____

_____

DAY 59

I fully acknowledge and I am grateful
for divine abundance in my life.

♡ ♡ ♡ ♡ ♡

Set your intentions for the day by...

Repeating the affirmation

_____

_____

_____

Thinking and writing positive thoughts

_____

_____

_____

Loving yourself

_____

_____

_____

DAY 60

Blessings of divine abundance create miracles
in my life. I am grateful for these gifts.

♡ ♡ ♡ ♡ ♡

Set your intentions for the day by...

Repeating the affirmation

_____

_____

_____

Thinking and writing positive thoughts

_____

_____

_____

Loving yourself

_____

_____

_____

DAY 61

I am grateful for success, prosperity,
and divine abundance in my life.

♡ ♡ ♡ ♡ ♡

Set your intentions for the day by...

Repeating the affirmation

_____

_____

_____

Thinking and writing positive thoughts

_____

_____

_____

Loving yourself

_____

_____

_____

DAY 62

I affirm that my vibration is a perfect match for
divine abundance. I am grateful for it all.

♡ ♡ ♡ ♡ ♡

Set your intentions for the day by...

Repeating the affirmation

_____

_____

_____

Thinking and writing positive thoughts

_____

_____

_____

Loving yourself

_____

_____

_____

DAY 63

I believe in miracles. I am grateful and
I am fully open to accept divine abundance.

♡ ♡ ♡ ♡ ♡

Set your intentions for the day by...

Repeating the affirmation

_____

_____

_____

Thinking and writing positive thoughts

_____

_____

_____

Loving yourself

_____

_____

_____

DAY 64

Manifesting divine abundance flows from an open heart. My heart is open. I am grateful for all.

♡ ♡ ♡ ♡ ♡

Set your intentions for the day by...

Repeating the affirmation

_____

_____

_____

Thinking and writing positive thoughts

_____

_____

_____

Loving yourself

_____

_____

_____

DAY 65

Divine abundance showers down on me like
rain. I am grateful to be in this flow.

$\heartsuit$ $\heartsuit$ $\heartsuit$ $\heartsuit$ $\heartsuit$

Set your intentions for the day by...

Repeating the affirmation

_____

_____

_____

Thinking and writing positive thoughts

_____

_____

_____

Loving yourself

_____

_____

_____

DAY 66

My thoughts, words, and deeds align me
for success, prosperity, and divine abundance.
I am grateful for all that I have.

♡ ♡ ♡ ♡ ♡

Set your intentions for the day by...

Repeating the affirmation

_____

_____

_____

Thinking and writing positive thoughts

_____

_____

_____

Loving yourself

_____

_____

_____

DAY 67

I am grateful for the manifestation of success, prosperity, and divine abundance in my life.

♡   ♡   ♡   ♡   ♡

Set your intentions for the day by...

Repeating the affirmation

_____

_____

_____

Thinking and writing positive thoughts

_____

_____

_____

Loving yourself

_____

_____

_____

DAY 68

I have more than enough in my life to meet
and surpass my every need. I am grateful that
I am graced with divine abundance.

♡　♡　♡　♡　♡

Set your intentions for the day by...

Repeating the affirmation

_____

_____

_____

Thinking and writing positive thoughts

_____

_____

_____

Loving yourself

_____

_____

_____

DAY 69

Divine abundance multiplies each and everyday.
I am grateful for the abundance that I receive.

♡   ♡   ♡   ♡   ♡

Set your intentions for the day by...

Repeating the affirmation

_____

_____

_____

Thinking and writing positive thoughts

_____

_____

_____

Loving yourself

_____

_____

_____

DAY 70

I am aligned with divine abundance.
Each day I am gifted with incredible success,
prosperity, and wealth. I am grateful.

♡　♡　♡　♡　♡

Set your intentions for the day by...

Repeating the affirmation

_____

_____

_____

Thinking and writing positive thoughts

_____

_____

_____

Loving yourself

_____

_____

_____

DAY 71

Gratitude is the key to divine abundance.
Thank you! Thank you! Thank you!

♡　♡　♡　♡　♡

Set your intentions for the day by...

Repeating the affirmation

_____

_____

_____

Thinking and writing positive thoughts

_____

_____

_____

Loving yourself

_____

_____

_____

DAY 72

I am grateful that divine abundance
is all around me.

♡　♡　♡　♡　♡

Set your intentions for the day by...

Repeating the affirmation

_____

_____

_____

Thinking and writing positive thoughts

_____

_____

_____

Loving yourself

_____

_____

_____

DAY 73

I experience powerful changes in my life
through divine abundance and gratitude.

♡   ♡   ♡   ♡   ♡

Set your intentions for the day by...

Repeating the affirmation

_____

_____

_____

Thinking and writing positive thoughts

_____

_____

_____

Loving yourself

_____

_____

_____

DAY 74

I am a magnet for divine abundance, success, and prosperity. I am grateful for all that I have.

♡ ♡ ♡ ♡ ♡

Set your intentions for the day by...

Repeating the affirmation

_____

_____

_____

Thinking and writing positive thoughts

_____

_____

_____

Loving yourself

_____

_____

_____

DAY 75

I am open to the flow of divine abundance in all that I do. I give thanks, love, and gratitude for all that I have been gifted.

♡　♡　♡　♡　♡

Set your intentions for the day by...

Repeating the affirmation

_____

_____

_____

Thinking and writing positive thoughts

_____

_____

_____

Loving yourself

_____

_____

_____

DAY 76

I am grateful. I am thankful.
I am aligned with divine abundance.

♡ ♡ ♡ ♡ ♡

Set your intentions for the day by...

Repeating the affirmation

_____

_____

_____

Thinking and writing positive thoughts

_____

_____

_____

Loving yourself

_____

_____

_____

DAY 77

Miracles and divine abundance are present in
my life. I am thankful and grateful for all that
I experience on a daily basis.

♡   ♡   ♡   ♡   ♡

Set your intentions for the day by...

Repeating the affirmation

_____

_____

_____

Thinking and writing positive thoughts

_____

_____

_____

Loving yourself

_____

_____

_____

DAY 78

I am a being of love. I am a being of light.
I am grateful that divine abundance
flows easily and effortlessly into my life.

♡   ♡   ♡   ♡   ♡

Set your intentions for the day by...

Repeating the affirmation

_____

_____

_____

Thinking and writing positive thoughts

_____

_____

_____

Loving yourself

_____

_____

_____

DAY 79

Divine abundance and gratitude
are key components in my life.
I am blessed with all that it brings to me.

♡　♡　♡　♡　♡

Set your intentions for the day by...

Repeating the affirmation

_____

_____

_____

Thinking and writing positive thoughts

_____

_____

_____

Loving yourself

_____

_____

_____

DAY 80

I am blessed each day by success. I am grateful
that divine abundance is present in my life.

♡　♡　♡　♡　♡

Set your intentions for the day by...

Repeating the affirmation

_____

_____

_____

Thinking and writing positive thoughts

_____

_____

_____

Loving yourself

_____

_____

_____

DAY 81

Divine abundance is all around me.
I am grateful for the immediate manifestation
that is occurring with me.

♡ ♡ ♡ ♡ ♡

Set your intentions for the day by...

Repeating the affirmation

_____

_____

_____

Thinking and writing positive thoughts

_____

_____

_____

Loving yourself

_____

_____

_____

DAY 82

Gratitude and appreciation create divine
abundance in all areas of my life.

♡ ♡ ♡ ♡ ♡

Set your intentions for the day by...

Repeating the affirmation

_____

_____

_____

Thinking and writing positive thoughts

_____

_____

_____

Loving yourself

_____

_____

_____

DAY 83

I am grateful that I manifest divine
abundance into my life.

♡　♡　♡　♡　♡

Set your intentions for the day by...

Repeating the affirmation

_____

_____

_____

Thinking and writing positive thoughts

_____

_____

_____

Loving yourself

_____

_____

_____

DAY 84

I attract the very best around me and manifest divine abundance, prosperity, and success in my life.
I am grateful for the blessings.

♡ ♡ ♡ ♡ ♡

Set your intentions for the day by...

Repeating the affirmation

_____

_____

_____

Thinking and writing positive thoughts

_____

_____

_____

Loving yourself

_____

_____

_____

DAY 85

I appreciate and I am grateful for the
divine abundance that surrounds me.

♡   ♡   ♡   ♡   ♡

Set your intentions for the day by...

Repeating the affirmation

_____

_____

_____

Thinking and writing positive thoughts

_____

_____

_____

Loving yourself

_____

_____

_____

DAY 86

Every day, in every way, I am manifesting divine abundance in my life. I am grateful.

♡ ♡ ♡ ♡ ♡

Set your intentions for the day by...

Repeating the affirmation

_____

_____

_____

Thinking and writing positive thoughts

_____

_____

_____

Loving yourself

_____

_____

_____

DAY 87

Appreciation, gratitude, and a loving heart
manifest divine abundance in infinite amounts.

♡ ♡ ♡ ♡ ♡

Set your intentions for the day by...

Repeating the affirmation

_____

_____

_____

Thinking and writing positive thoughts

_____

_____

_____

Loving yourself

_____

_____

_____

DAY 88

I am grateful for the divine abundance
that has blessed my life.

♡ ♡ ♡ ♡ ♡

Set your intentions for the day by...

Repeating the affirmation

_____

_____

_____

Thinking and writing positive thoughts

_____

_____

_____

Loving yourself

_____

_____

_____

DAY 89

Divine abundance is available to me and for me.
I am grateful.

♡ ♡ ♡ ♡ ♡

Set your intentions for the day by...

Repeating the affirmation

_____

_____

_____

Thinking and writing positive thoughts

_____

_____

_____

Loving yourself

_____

_____

_____

DAY 90

Every day, in every way, I experience divine abundance in my life. I am grateful for the opportunities it brings.

♡ ♡ ♡ ♡ ♡

Set your intentions for the day by...

Repeating the affirmation

_____

_____

_____

Thinking and writing positive thoughts

_____

_____

_____

Loving yourself

_____

_____

_____

DAY 91

I am in awe of the blessings and divine abundance
that I receive each day. I am grateful.

♡　♡　♡　♡　♡

Set your intentions for the day by...

Repeating the affirmation

_____

_____

_____

Thinking and writing positive thoughts

_____

_____

_____

Loving yourself

_____

_____

_____

DAY 92

Success, prosperity, and divine abundance are part of my life. I create more and more each day through gratitude.

♡　♡　♡　♡　♡

Set your intentions for the day by...

Repeating the affirmation

_____

_____

_____

Thinking and writing positive thoughts

_____

_____

_____

Loving yourself

_____

_____

_____

DAY 93

My heart sings with joy and gratitude
for the divine abundance in my life.

♡ ♡ ♡ ♡ ♡

Set your intentions for the day by...

Repeating the affirmation

_____

_____

_____

Thinking and writing positive thoughts

_____

_____

_____

Loving yourself

_____

_____

_____

DAY 94

Divine abundance is easy and manifests miracles
in my life. I am grateful for all that I have.

♡　♡　♡　♡　♡

Set your intentions for the day by...

Repeating the affirmation

_____

_____

_____

Thinking and writing positive thoughts

_____

_____

_____

Loving yourself

_____

_____

_____

DAY 95

Divine abundance flows with my thoughts. I am grateful for all that has been created in my life.

♡　♡　♡　♡　♡

Set your intentions for the day by...

Repeating the affirmation

_____

_____

_____

Thinking and writing positive thoughts

_____

_____

_____

Loving yourself

_____

_____

_____

DAY 96

Each morning I wake to the manifestation of divine abundance. I am grateful for all that it has brought me.

♡ ♡ ♡ ♡ ♡

Set your intentions for the day by...

Repeating the affirmation

_____

_____

_____

Thinking and writing positive thoughts

_____

_____

_____

Loving yourself

_____

_____

_____

DAY 97

Divine abundance is birthed out of gratitude.
I am blessed and grateful for all that I have.

♡ ♡ ♡ ♡ ♡

Set your intentions for the day by...

Repeating the affirmation

_____

_____

_____

Thinking and writing positive thoughts

_____

_____

_____

Loving yourself

_____

_____

_____

DAY 98

Love and gratitude create the miracle of divine
abundance in my life and I am grateful.

♡   ♡   ♡   ♡   ♡

Set your intentions for the day by...

Repeating the affirmation

_____

_____

_____

Thinking and writing positive thoughts

_____

_____

_____

Loving yourself

_____

_____

_____

DAY 99

I am grateful for the divine abundance, success, wealth, and prosperity that bless my life.

♡ ♡ ♡ ♡ ♡

Set your intentions for the day by...

Repeating the affirmation

_____

_____

_____

Thinking and writing positive thoughts

_____

_____

_____

Loving yourself

_____

_____

_____

DAY 100

With gratitude, I expect miracles and divine abundance in my life each day.

♡   ♡   ♡   ♡   ♡

Set your intentions for the day by...

Repeating the affirmation

_____

_____

_____

Thinking and writing positive thoughts

_____

_____

_____

Loving yourself

_____

_____

_____

DAY 101

Love, blessings, miracles, and divine
abundance surround me and I am grateful.

$\heartsuit$ $\heartsuit$ $\heartsuit$ $\heartsuit$ $\heartsuit$

Set your intentions for the day by...

Repeating the affirmation

_____

_____

_____

Thinking and writing positive thoughts

_____

_____

_____

Loving yourself

_____

_____

_____

DAY 102

I live my life with gratitude for all that I have
and all that I am. Divine abundance is my life.

♡   ♡   ♡   ♡   ♡

Set your intentions for the day by...

Repeating the affirmation

_____

_____

_____

Thinking and writing positive thoughts

_____

_____

_____

Loving yourself

_____

_____

_____

DAY 103

Thank you, thank you, thank you. My heart is filled with gratitude for the divine abundance in my life.

♡ ♡ ♡ ♡ ♡

Set your intentions for the day by...

Repeating the affirmation

_____

_____

_____

Thinking and writing positive thoughts

_____

_____

_____

Loving yourself

_____

_____

_____

DAY 104

Each and every day I am amazed how I am graced with divine abundance. I am grateful for all that I have.

♡　♡　♡　♡　♡

Set your intentions for the day by...

Repeating the affirmation

_____

_____

_____

Thinking and writing positive thoughts

_____

_____

_____

Loving yourself

_____

_____

_____

DAY 105

Divine inspiration, divine abundance,
and gratitude are reflected in my life.

♡   ♡   ♡   ♡   ♡

Set your intentions for the day by...

Repeating the affirmation

_____

_____

_____

Thinking and writing positive thoughts

_____

_____

_____

Loving yourself

_____

_____

_____

DAY 106

I am grateful that divine abundance is reflected
in everything that I do and all that I am.

♡   ♡   ♡   ♡   ♡

Set your intentions for the day by...

Repeating the affirmation

_____

_____

_____

Thinking and writing positive thoughts

_____

_____

_____

Loving yourself

_____

_____

_____

DAY 107

I am grateful for the flow of divine abundance in my life. I am blessed in miraculous ways.

♡ ♡ ♡ ♡ ♡

Set your intentions for the day by...

Repeating the affirmation

_____

_____

_____

Thinking and writing positive thoughts

_____

_____

_____

Loving yourself

_____

_____

_____

DAY 108

Each day new blessings and divine
abundance flow into my life and I am grateful.

♡ ♡ ♡ ♡ ♡

Set your intentions for the day by...

Repeating the affirmation

_____

_____

_____

Thinking and writing positive thoughts

_____

_____

_____

Loving yourself

_____

_____

_____

DAY 109

I am grateful for the spectacular day.
Divine abundance is all around me in everything I do.

♡ ♡ ♡ ♡ ♡

Set your intentions for the day by...

Repeating the affirmation

_____

_____

_____

Thinking and writing positive thoughts

_____

_____

_____

Loving yourself

_____

_____

_____

DAY 110

I am grateful for each and every gift that
I receive created through divine abundance.

♡ ♡ ♡ ♡ ♡

Set your intentions for the day by...

Repeating the affirmation

_____

_____

_____

Thinking and writing positive thoughts

_____

_____

_____

Loving yourself

_____

_____

_____

DAY 111

My heart is pure, open, and filled with gratitude for divine abundance and all the gifts that I am blessed with.

♡ ♡ ♡ ♡ ♡

Set your intentions for the day by...

Repeating the affirmation

_____

_____

_____

Thinking and writing positive thoughts

_____

_____

_____

Loving yourself

_____

_____

_____

DAY 112

Love leads me to the light and gratitude
creates divine abundance in my life.

♡ ♡ ♡ ♡ ♡

Set your intentions for the day by...

Repeating the affirmation

_____

_____

_____

Thinking and writing positive thoughts

_____

_____

_____

Loving yourself

_____

_____

_____

DAY 113

My thoughts are of love and light. This creates success, prosperity, and divine abundance in my life.

♡   ♡   ♡   ♡   ♡

Set your intentions for the day by...

Repeating the affirmation

_____

_____

_____

Thinking and writing positive thoughts

_____

_____

_____

Loving yourself

_____

_____

_____

DAY 114

I am guided each day with divine presence and gifted with divine abundance. I am grateful for this in my life.

♡ ♡ ♡ ♡ ♡

Set your intentions for the day by...

Repeating the affirmation

_____

_____

_____

Thinking and writing positive thoughts

_____

_____

_____

Loving yourself

_____

_____

_____

DAY 115

Divine abundance is always present in my life and
I am grateful that anything and everything is possible.

♡ ♡ ♡ ♡ ♡

Set your intentions for the day by...

Repeating the affirmation

_____

_____

_____

Thinking and writing positive thoughts

_____

_____

_____

Loving yourself

_____

_____

_____

DAY 116

Gratitude brings more and more
divine abundance everyday.

♡　♡　♡　♡　♡

Set your intentions for the day by...

Repeating the affirmation

_____

_____

_____

Thinking and writing positive thoughts

_____

_____

_____

Loving yourself

_____

_____

_____

DAY 117

I breathe in love and light and exhale gratitude
for the divine abundance that touches my life.

♡ ♡ ♡ ♡ ♡

Set your intentions for the day by...

Repeating the affirmation

_____

_____

_____

Thinking and writing positive thoughts

_____

_____

_____

Loving yourself

_____

_____

_____

DAY 118

There are infinite quantities of divine abundance
that flow into my life. I am grateful for the possibilities.

♡ ♡ ♡ ♡ ♡

Set your intentions for the day by...

Repeating the affirmation

_____

_____

_____

Thinking and writing positive thoughts

_____

_____

_____

Loving yourself

_____

_____

_____

DAY 119

I love, love, love, that I am blessed with divine abundance.
Gratitude freely flows in appreciation and thanks.

♡ ♡ ♡ ♡ ♡

Set your intentions for the day by...

Repeating the affirmation

_____

_____

_____

Thinking and writing positive thoughts

_____

_____

_____

Loving yourself

_____

_____

_____

DAY 120

I am grateful for the miracle of
divine abundance in my life.

♡ ♡ ♡ ♡ ♡

Set your intentions for the day by...

Repeating the affirmation

_____

_____

_____

Thinking and writing positive thoughts

_____

_____

_____

Loving yourself

_____

_____

_____

DAY 121

I am grateful for the presence of
divine abundance in my life.

♡   ♡   ♡   ♡   ♡

Set your intentions for the day by...

Repeating the affirmation

_____

_____

_____

Thinking and writing positive thoughts

_____

_____

_____

Loving yourself

_____

_____

_____

DAY 122

I am blessed by divine abundance
and I am grateful.

♡　♡　♡　♡　♡

Set your intentions for the day by...

Repeating the affirmation

_____

_____

_____

Thinking and writing positive thoughts

_____

_____

_____

Loving yourself

_____

_____

_____

DAY 123

I live my life in gratitude knowing divine
abundance is all around me.

♡　♡　♡　♡　♡

Set your intentions for the day by...

Repeating the affirmation

_____

_____

_____

Thinking and writing positive thoughts

_____

_____

_____

Loving yourself

_____

_____

_____

DAY 124

I am inspired each day to be my best self, to be grateful,
and to know that divine abundance flows into my life.

♡ ♡ ♡ ♡ ♡

Set your intentions for the day by...

Repeating the affirmation

_____

_____

_____

Thinking and writing positive thoughts

_____

_____

_____

Loving yourself

_____

_____

_____

DAY 125

I am grateful for divine abundance, prosperity, and success in all aspects of my life. I easily manifest all that I desire.

♡ ♡ ♡ ♡ ♡

Set your intentions for the day by...

Repeating the affirmation

_____

_____

_____

Thinking and writing positive thoughts

_____

_____

_____

Loving yourself

_____

_____

_____

DAY 126

Divine abundance overflows creating infinite amounts prosperity in my life. I am grateful.

♡ ♡ ♡ ♡ ♡

Set your intentions for the day by...

Repeating the affirmation

_____

_____

_____

Thinking and writing positive thoughts

_____

_____

_____

Loving yourself

_____

_____

_____

DAY 127

I am grateful that divine abundance flows to me,
through me, and is a part of my every day life.

♡ ♡ ♡ ♡ ♡

Set your intentions for the day by...

Repeating the affirmation

_____

_____

_____

Thinking and writing positive thoughts

_____

_____

_____

Loving yourself

_____

_____

_____

DAY 128

I am grateful that there is a constant flow of divine abundance manifesting in my life.

♡ ♡ ♡ ♡ ♡

Set your intentions for the day by...

Repeating the affirmation

_____

_____

_____

Thinking and writing positive thoughts

_____

_____

_____

Loving yourself

_____

_____

_____

DAY 129

I am eternally grateful for the divine
abundance that blesses my life.

♡ ♡ ♡ ♡ ♡

Set your intentions for the day by...

Repeating the affirmation

_____

_____

_____

Thinking and writing positive thoughts

_____

_____

_____

Loving yourself

_____

_____

_____

DAY 130

I am aware and I am grateful for the success, prosperity, and divine abundance that manifests in my life daily.

♡ ♡ ♡ ♡ ♡

Set your intentions for the day by...

Repeating the affirmation

_____

_____

_____

Thinking and writing positive thoughts

_____

_____

_____

Loving yourself

_____

_____

_____

DAY 131

Miracles bless my life and I manifest divine abundance.
I am grateful for the opportunities this brings.

♡ ♡ ♡ ♡ ♡

Set your intentions for the day by...

Repeating the affirmation

_____

_____

_____

Thinking and writing positive thoughts

_____

_____

_____

Loving yourself

_____

_____

_____

DAY 132

I am grateful, successful, and prosperous for
the divine abundance that graces my life.

♡ ♡ ♡ ♡ ♡

Set your intentions for the day by...

Repeating the affirmation

_____

_____

_____

Thinking and writing positive thoughts

_____

_____

_____

Loving yourself

_____

_____

_____

DAY 133

Sparks of divinity flow to me, through me, and around me.
My life overflows with divine abundance. I am grateful.

♡ ♡ ♡ ♡ ♡

Set your intentions for the day by...

Repeating the affirmation

_____

_____

_____

Thinking and writing positive thoughts

_____

_____

_____

Loving yourself

_____

_____

_____

DAY 134

I am never alone. Divine presence graces my life
and divine abundance abounds.
I am grateful for all that I am and all that I have.

♡   ♡   ♡   ♡   ♡

Set your intentions for the day by...

Repeating the affirmation

_____

_____

_____

Thinking and writing positive thoughts

_____

_____

_____

Loving yourself

_____

_____

_____

DAY 135

I am grateful each day for the divine
abundance that blesses my life.

♡　♡　♡　♡　♡

Set your intentions for the day by...

Repeating the affirmation

_____

_____

_____

Thinking and writing positive thoughts

_____

_____

_____

Loving yourself

_____

_____

_____

DAY 136

I am grateful that I have infinite amounts of love and divine abundance in my life.

♡　♡　♡　♡　♡

Set your intentions for the day by...

Repeating the affirmation

_____

_____

_____

Thinking and writing positive thoughts

_____

_____

_____

Loving yourself

_____

_____

_____

DAY 137

I am grateful for the manifestation of divine abundance, success, and prosperity in my life.

♡ ♡ ♡ ♡ ♡

Set your intentions for the day by...

Repeating the affirmation

_____

_____

_____

Thinking and writing positive thoughts

_____

_____

_____

Loving yourself

_____

_____

_____

DAY 138

My life is full of happiness, joy, peace, contentment,
and divine abundance. I am grateful for all that I have.

♡ ♡ ♡ ♡ ♡

Set your intentions for the day by...

Repeating the affirmation

_____

_____

_____

Thinking and writing positive thoughts

_____

_____

_____

Loving yourself

_____

_____

_____

DAY 139

Gratitude has brought success, prosperity,
and divine abundance to me.

♡ ♡ ♡ ♡ ♡

Set your intentions for the day by...

Repeating the affirmation

_____

_____

_____

Thinking and writing positive thoughts

_____

_____

_____

Loving yourself

_____

_____

_____

DAY 140

I am grateful that I manifest divine
abundance now and always in my life.

♡   ♡   ♡   ♡   ♡

Set your intentions for the day by...

Repeating the affirmation

_____

_____

_____

Thinking and writing positive thoughts

_____

_____

_____

Loving yourself

_____

_____

_____

DAY 141

Divine abundance surrounds me
and I am grateful.

♡ ♡ ♡ ♡ ♡

Set your intentions for the day by...

Repeating the affirmation

_____

_____

_____

Thinking and writing positive thoughts

_____

_____

_____

Loving yourself

_____

_____

_____

DAY 142

I manifest success, prosperity, and
divine abundance in my life. I am grateful.

♡ ♡ ♡ ♡ ♡

Set your intentions for the day by...

Repeating the affirmation

_____

_____

_____

Thinking and writing positive thoughts

_____

_____

_____

Loving yourself

_____

_____

_____

DAY 143

I deserve prosperity and divine abundance,
and I am grateful for all that I receive.

♡ ♡ ♡ ♡ ♡

Set your intentions for the day by...

Repeating the affirmation

_____

_____

_____

Thinking and writing positive thoughts

_____

_____

_____

Loving yourself

_____

_____

_____

DAY 144

I attract divine abundance into my life
with gratitude and love.

♡　♡　♡　♡　♡

Set your intentions for the day by...

Repeating the affirmation

_____

_____

_____

Thinking and writing positive thoughts

_____

_____

_____

Loving yourself

_____

_____

_____

DAY 145

I draw divine abundance easily and effortlessly into my life, and I am grateful for all that I receive.

♡ ♡ ♡ ♡ ♡

Set your intentions for the day by...

Repeating the affirmation

_____

_____

_____

Thinking and writing positive thoughts

_____

_____

_____

Loving yourself

_____

_____

_____

DAY 146

I accept divine abundance and all
that it brings to me with gratitude.

♡ ♡ ♡ ♡ ♡

Set your intentions for the day by...

Repeating the affirmation

_____

_____

_____

Thinking and writing positive thoughts

_____

_____

_____

Loving yourself

_____

_____

_____

DAY 147

Gratitude and love bring forth
divine abundance in my life.

♡ ♡ ♡ ♡ ♡

Set your intentions for the day by...

Repeating the affirmation

_____

_____

_____

Thinking and writing positive thoughts

_____

_____

_____

Loving yourself

_____

_____

_____

DAY 148

I am thankful and grateful for the beautiful gift
of divine abundance that touches my life.

♡ ♡ ♡ ♡ ♡

Set your intentions for the day by...

Repeating the affirmation

_____

_____

_____

Thinking and writing positive thoughts

_____

_____

_____

Loving yourself

_____

_____

_____

DAY 149

Divine abundance in my life, is the result of gratitude, love and positive thoughts. All good things manifest for me.

♡ ♡ ♡ ♡ ♡

Set your intentions for the day by...

Repeating the affirmation

_____

_____

_____

Thinking and writing positive thoughts

_____

_____

_____

Loving yourself

_____

_____

_____

DAY 150

I am grateful that I draw divine abundance into my life
with loving, positive, thoughts, words, and deeds.

♡ ♡ ♡ ♡ ♡

Set your intentions for the day by...

Repeating the affirmation

_____

_____

_____

Thinking and writing positive thoughts

_____

_____

_____

Loving yourself

_____

_____

_____

DAY 151

Success, prosperity, and divine abundance are the outward signs of my grateful heart.

♡ ♡ ♡ ♡ ♡

Set your intentions for the day by...

Repeating the affirmation

_____

_____

_____

Thinking and writing positive thoughts

_____

_____

_____

Loving yourself

_____

_____

_____

DAY 152

I am grateful divine abundance and
all good things come to me now.

♡　♡　♡　♡　♡

Set your intentions for the day by...

Repeating the affirmation

_____

_____

_____

Thinking and writing positive thoughts

_____

_____

_____

Loving yourself

_____

_____

_____

DAY 153

Divine abundance is my birthright
and I gratefully accept all of it now.

♡　♡　♡　♡　♡

Set your intentions for the day by...

Repeating the affirmation

_____

_____

_____

Thinking and writing positive thoughts

_____

_____

_____

Loving yourself

_____

_____

_____

DAY 154

I am grateful and thankful for the flow
of divine abundance in my life.

♡　♡　♡　♡　♡

Set your intentions for the day by...

Repeating the affirmation

_____

_____

_____

Thinking and writing positive thoughts

_____

_____

_____

Loving yourself

_____

_____

_____

DAY 155

Divine abundance easily and effortlessly flows to me
and blesses my life. I am grateful for all it brings.

♡ ♡ ♡ ♡ ♡

Set your intentions for the day by...

Repeating the affirmation

_____

_____

_____

Thinking and writing positive thoughts

_____

_____

_____

Loving yourself

_____

_____

_____

DAY 156

I am grateful for being blessed by
miracles and divine abundance.

♡ ♡ ♡ ♡ ♡

Set your intentions for the day by...

Repeating the affirmation

_____

_____

_____

Thinking and writing positive thoughts

_____

_____

_____

Loving yourself

_____

_____

_____

DAY 157

I am grateful and I love, love, love, that
divine abundance is all around me.

♡ ♡ ♡ ♡ ♡

Set your intentions for the day by...

Repeating the affirmation

_____

_____

_____

Thinking and writing positive thoughts

_____

_____

_____

Loving yourself

_____

_____

_____

DAY 158

I am a magnet for all good things and for the flow of divine abundance into my life. I am grateful for the positive impact it has on me.

♡ ♡ ♡ ♡ ♡

Set your intentions for the day by...

Repeating the affirmation

_____

_____

_____

Thinking and writing positive thoughts

_____

_____

_____

Loving yourself

_____

_____

_____

DAY 159

I am surrounded in bliss and divine abundance.
I am grateful each day for what manifests in my life.

♡ ♡ ♡ ♡ ♡

Set your intentions for the day by...

Repeating the affirmation

_____

_____

_____

Thinking and writing positive thoughts

_____

_____

_____

Loving yourself

_____

_____

_____

DAY 160

I am a magnet for divine abundance. I am grateful
and thankful for all that I am and all that I have.

♡ ♡ ♡ ♡ ♡

Set your intentions for the day by...

Repeating the affirmation

_____

_____

_____

Thinking and writing positive thoughts

_____

_____

_____

Loving yourself

_____

_____

_____

DAY 161

I am grateful for the divine abundance
that is always present in my life.

♡ ♡ ♡ ♡ ♡

Set your intentions for the day by...

Repeating the affirmation

_____

_____

_____

Thinking and writing positive thoughts

_____

_____

_____

Loving yourself

_____

_____

_____

DAY 162

Divine abundance is always available to me.
It touches my life in countless ways and
I am grateful for everything that I have.

♡ ♡ ♡ ♡ ♡

Set your intentions for the day by...

Repeating the affirmation

_____

_____

_____

Thinking and writing positive thoughts

_____

_____

_____

Loving yourself

_____

_____

_____

DAY 163

My internal light shines brightly as I show
gratitude and thanks for the manifestation of
divine abundance and all good things in my life.

♡　♡　♡　♡　♡

Set your intentions for the day by...

Repeating the affirmation

_____

_____

_____

Thinking and writing positive thoughts

_____

_____

_____

Loving yourself

_____

_____

_____

DAY 164

Divine abundance rocks my life.
I am grateful for all that flows to me.

♡　♡　♡　♡　♡

Set your intentions for the day by...

Repeating the affirmation

_____

_____

_____

Thinking and writing positive thoughts

_____

_____

_____

Loving yourself

_____

_____

_____

DAY 165

Love and gratitude is the key for the
manifestation of divine abundance in my life.

♡　♡　♡　♡　♡

Set your intentions for the day by...

Repeating the affirmation

_____

_____

_____

Thinking and writing positive thoughts

_____

_____

_____

Loving yourself

_____

_____

_____

DAY 166

My heart is filled with gratitude, joy, and happiness for the divine abundance that is in my life.

♡ ♡ ♡ ♡ ♡

Set your intentions for the day by...

Repeating the affirmation

_____

_____

_____

Thinking and writing positive thoughts

_____

_____

_____

Loving yourself

_____

_____

_____

DAY 167

I am open and I accept the flow of divine abundance in my life. I am grateful for all that is provided.

♡ ♡ ♡ ♡ ♡

Set your intentions for the day by...

Repeating the affirmation

_____

_____

_____

Thinking and writing positive thoughts

_____

_____

_____

Loving yourself

_____

_____

_____

DAY 168

I am grateful that divine abundance is always part of my life. My thoughts, words, and deeds have opened me to the constant flow.

♡　♡　♡　♡　♡

Set your intentions for the day by...

Repeating the affirmation

_____

_____

_____

Thinking and writing positive thoughts

_____

_____

_____

Loving yourself

_____

_____

_____

DAY 169

I am grateful for the opportunities that divine abundance brings to me each and every day.

♡ ♡ ♡ ♡ ♡

Set your intentions for the day by...

Repeating the affirmation

_____

_____

_____

Thinking and writing positive thoughts

_____

_____

_____

Loving yourself

_____

_____

_____

DAY 170

I am secure in knowing that divine abundance is all around me and I am grateful for its presence in my life.

♡ ♡ ♡ ♡ ♡

Set your intentions for the day by...

Repeating the affirmation

_____

_____

_____

Thinking and writing positive thoughts

_____

_____

_____

Loving yourself

_____

_____

_____

DAY 171

Today I give thanks and I express my gratitude for the divine abundance that surrounds my being and is part of my life.

♡ ♡ ♡ ♡ ♡

Set your intentions for the day by...

Repeating the affirmation

_____

_____

_____

Thinking and writing positive thoughts

_____

_____

_____

Loving yourself

_____

_____

_____

DAY 172

My gratitude and my thanks have kept me in a
constant flow of divine abundance.

♡ ♡ ♡ ♡ ♡

Set your intentions for the day by...

Repeating the affirmation

_____

_____

_____

Thinking and writing positive thoughts

_____

_____

_____

Loving yourself

_____

_____

_____

DAY 173

Divine abundance flows to me and creates
miracles in my life. I am grateful.

♡ ♡ ♡ ♡ ♡

Set your intentions for the day by...

Repeating the affirmation

_____

_____

_____

Thinking and writing positive thoughts

_____

_____

_____

Loving yourself

_____

_____

_____

DAY 174

Divine abundance is always available
to me through gratitude.

♡   ♡   ♡   ♡   ♡

Set your intentions for the day by...

Repeating the affirmation

_____

_____

_____

Thinking and writing positive thoughts

_____

_____

_____

Loving yourself

_____

_____

_____

DAY 175

I am grateful and I count my blessings
for the divine abundance in my life.

♡　♡　♡　♡　♡

Set your intentions for the day by...

Repeating the affirmation

_____

_____

_____

Thinking and writing positive thoughts

_____

_____

_____

Loving yourself

_____

_____

_____

DAY 176

I am grateful for the divine abundance
that is always present in my life.

♡ ♡ ♡ ♡ ♡

Set your intentions for the day by...

Repeating the affirmation

_____

_____

_____

Thinking and writing positive thoughts

_____

_____

_____

Loving yourself

_____

_____

_____

DAY 177

I am aligned for success, prosperity, wealth,
and divine abundance and I am grateful.

♡ ♡ ♡ ♡ ♡

Set your intentions for the day by...

Repeating the affirmation

_____

_____

_____

Thinking and writing positive thoughts

_____

_____

_____

Loving yourself

_____

_____

_____

DAY 178

I am grateful for all the opportunities that
have been provided through divine abundance
and my connection with all there is.

♡ ♡ ♡ ♡ ♡

Set your intentions for the day by...

Repeating the affirmation

_____

_____

_____

Thinking and writing positive thoughts

_____

_____

_____

Loving yourself

_____

_____

_____

DAY 179

The Universe provides infinite amounts of divine abundance.
The flow is constant and always plentiful. I am grateful.

♡   ♡   ♡   ♡   ♡

Set your intentions for the day by...

Repeating the affirmation

_____

_____

_____

Thinking and writing positive thoughts

_____

_____

_____

Loving yourself

_____

_____

_____

DAY 180

I give thanks and gratitude each day
for divine abundance. I am blessed.

♡　♡　♡　♡　♡

Set your intentions for the day by...

Repeating the affirmation

_____

_____

_____

Thinking and writing positive thoughts

_____

_____

_____

Loving yourself

_____

_____

_____

DAY 181

There is always more than enough
divine abundance. I am grateful.

♡ ♡ ♡ ♡ ♡

Set your intentions for the day by...

Repeating the affirmation

_____

_____

_____

Thinking and writing positive thoughts

_____

_____

_____

Loving yourself

_____

_____

_____

DAY 182

I am grateful that divine abundance flows in,
through, and around me in constant flow.

♡ ♡ ♡ ♡ ♡

Set your intentions for the day by...

Repeating the affirmation

_____

_____

_____

Thinking and writing positive thoughts

_____

_____

_____

Loving yourself

_____

_____

_____

DAY 183

Divine abundance is a state of mind. I always express my gratitude and appreciation with love.

♡　♡　♡　♡　♡

Set your intentions for the day by...

Repeating the affirmation

_____

_____

_____

Thinking and writing positive thoughts

_____

_____

_____

Loving yourself

_____

_____

_____

DAY 184

I am grateful for the manifestation
of divine abundance in my life.

♡　♡　♡　♡　♡

Set your intentions for the day by...

Repeating the affirmation

_____

_____

_____

Thinking and writing positive thoughts

_____

_____

_____

Loving yourself

_____

_____

_____

DAY 185

I am always and forever grateful for the
presence of divine abundance in my life.

♡　♡　♡　♡　♡

Set your intentions for the day by...

Repeating the affirmation

_____

_____

_____

Thinking and writing positive thoughts

_____

_____

_____

Loving yourself

_____

_____

_____

DAY 186

I am grateful and appreciate the opportunities for divine abundance in my life.

♡ ♡ ♡ ♡ ♡

Set your intentions for the day by...

Repeating the affirmation

_____

_____

_____

Thinking and writing positive thoughts

_____

_____

_____

Loving yourself

_____

_____

_____

DAY 187

The more my appreciation and gratitude flows with an open heart, the more I am blessed with divine abundance.

♡ ♡ ♡ ♡ ♡

Set your intentions for the day by...

Repeating the affirmation

_____

_____

_____

Thinking and writing positive thoughts

_____

_____

_____

Loving yourself

_____

_____

_____

DAY 188

Miracles bless my life on a daily basis. Divine abundance is one of those miracles and blessings. I am grateful.

♡ ♡ ♡ ♡ ♡

Set your intentions for the day by...

Repeating the affirmation

_____

_____

_____

Thinking and writing positive thoughts

_____

_____

_____

Loving yourself

_____

_____

_____

DAY 189

I am love. I am joy. I am grateful.
I create divine abundance around me.

♡   ♡   ♡   ♡   ♡

Set your intentions for the day by...

Repeating the affirmation

_____

_____

_____

Thinking and writing positive thoughts

_____

_____

_____

Loving yourself

_____

_____

_____

DAY 190

Divine abundance ripples out into my environment.
I am grateful for all good things that come to me now.

♡   ♡   ♡   ♡   ♡

Set your intentions for the day by...

Repeating the affirmation

_____

_____

_____

Thinking and writing positive thoughts

_____

_____

_____

Loving yourself

_____

_____

_____

DAY 191

I am successful, prosperous, grateful, and I experience divine abundance in my life.

♡　♡　♡　♡　♡

Set your intentions for the day by...

Repeating the affirmation

_____

_____

_____

Thinking and writing positive thoughts

_____

_____

_____

Loving yourself

_____

_____

_____

DAY 192

Divine abundance is my natural right.
I am grateful for all that it brings.

♡　♡　♡　♡　♡

Set your intentions for the day by...

Repeating the affirmation

_____

_____

_____

Thinking and writing positive thoughts

_____

_____

_____

Loving yourself

_____

_____

_____

DAY 193

I easily and effortlessly manifest divine
abundance in all areas of my life.
I am grateful for the changes that it brings.

♡ ♡ ♡ ♡ ♡

Set your intentions for the day by...

Repeating the affirmation

_____

_____

_____

Thinking and writing positive thoughts

_____

_____

_____

Loving yourself

_____

_____

_____

DAY 194

Divine abundance is my right. I am thankful
and grateful for the success, prosperity,
and wealth it has brought into my life.

♡　♡　♡　♡　♡

Set your intentions for the day by...

Repeating the affirmation

_____

_____

_____

Thinking and writing positive thoughts

_____

_____

_____

Loving yourself

_____

_____

_____

DAY 195

Divine abundance is created and manifested in my life. I easily and effortlessly attract what I need and I am grateful.

♡ ♡ ♡ ♡ ♡

Set your intentions for the day by...

Repeating the affirmation

_____

_____

_____

Thinking and writing positive thoughts

_____

_____

_____

Loving yourself

_____

_____

_____

DAY 196

Divine abundance surrounds me in all
areas of my life. I am grateful for all that is.

♡　♡　♡　♡　♡

Set your intentions for the day by...

Repeating the affirmation

_____

_____

_____

Thinking and writing positive thoughts

_____

_____

_____

Loving yourself

_____

_____

_____

DAY 197

I graciously and with gratitude accept
divine abundance and success into my life.

♡　♡　♡　♡　♡

Set your intentions for the day by...

Repeating the affirmation

_____

_____

_____

Thinking and writing positive thoughts

_____

_____

_____

Loving yourself

_____

_____

_____

DAY 198

I attract divine abundance into my life
through love and gratitude.

♡ ♡ ♡ ♡ ♡

Set your intentions for the day by...

Repeating the affirmation

_____

_____

_____

Thinking and writing positive thoughts

_____

_____

_____

Loving yourself

_____

_____

_____

DAY 199

I am grateful for the manifestation
of divine abundance in my life.

♡　♡　♡　♡　♡

Set your intentions for the day by...

Repeating the affirmation

_____

_____

_____

Thinking and writing positive thoughts

_____

_____

_____

Loving yourself

_____

_____

_____

DAY 200

I live in love, gratitude, and divine abundance.

♡ ♡ ♡ ♡ ♡

Set your intentions for the day by...

Repeating the affirmation

_____

_____

_____

Thinking and writing positive thoughts

_____

_____

_____

Loving yourself

_____

_____

_____

DAY 201

I choose to manifest divine abundance into my life
and I am grateful for all that has been created.

♡   ♡   ♡   ♡   ♡

Set your intentions for the day by...

Repeating the affirmation

_____

_____

_____

Thinking and writing positive thoughts

_____

_____

_____

Loving yourself

_____

_____

_____

DAY 202

I expect the miracle of divine abundance to manifest in my life through love, joy, happiness, and gratitude.

♡　♡　♡　♡　♡

Set your intentions for the day by...

Repeating the affirmation

_____

_____

_____

Thinking and writing positive thoughts

_____

_____

_____

Loving yourself

_____

_____

_____

DAY 203

I am grateful that everywhere I go,
divine abundance surrounds me.

♡　♡　♡　♡　♡

Set your intentions for the day by...

Repeating the affirmation

_____

_____

_____

Thinking and writing positive thoughts

_____

_____

_____

Loving yourself

_____

_____

_____

DAY 204

Gratitude brings miracles and
divine abundance to me.

♡　♡　♡　♡　♡

Set your intentions for the day by...

Repeating the affirmation

_____

_____

_____

Thinking and writing positive thoughts

_____

_____

_____

Loving yourself

_____

_____

_____

DAY 205

Gratitude unlocks the door to divine abundance
and divine abundance flows to me.

♡   ♡   ♡   ♡   ♡

Set your intentions for the day by...

Repeating the affirmation

_____

_____

_____

Thinking and writing positive thoughts

_____

_____

_____

Loving yourself

_____

_____

_____

DAY 206

I am open, receptive, and grateful for the blessing of divine abundance in my life.

♡　♡　♡　♡　♡

Set your intentions for the day by...

Repeating the affirmation

_____

_____

_____

Thinking and writing positive thoughts

_____

_____

_____

Loving yourself

_____

_____

_____

DAY 207

I gratefully create divine abundance in my life.

♡　♡　♡　♡　♡

Set your intentions for the day by...

Repeating the affirmation

_____

_____

_____

Thinking and writing positive thoughts

_____

_____

_____

Loving yourself

_____

_____

_____

DAY 208

I am blessed with divine abundance and grateful
for the changes that it has brought to my life.

♡ ♡ ♡ ♡ ♡

Set your intentions for the day by...

Repeating the affirmation

_____

_____

_____

Thinking and writing positive thoughts

_____

_____

_____

Loving yourself

_____

_____

_____

DAY 209

I am happy, excited, and grateful for the
divine abundance that flows to me.

♡　♡　♡　♡　♡

Set your intentions for the day by...

Repeating the affirmation

_____

_____

_____

Thinking and writing positive thoughts

_____

_____

_____

Loving yourself

_____

_____

_____

DAY 210

The light within me accepts the gifts
of divine abundance with gratitude.

♡ ♡ ♡ ♡ ♡

Set your intentions for the day by...

Repeating the affirmation

_____

_____

_____

Thinking and writing positive thoughts

_____

_____

_____

Loving yourself

_____

_____

_____

DAY 211

Divine abundance is everywhere
and with gratitude I accept it.

♡ ♡ ♡ ♡ ♡

Set your intentions for the day by...

Repeating the affirmation

_____

_____

_____

Thinking and writing positive thoughts

_____

_____

_____

Loving yourself

_____

_____

_____

DAY 212

Divine love brings divine abundance
into my life and I am grateful.

♡　♡　♡　♡　♡

Set your intentions for the day by...

Repeating the affirmation

_____

_____

_____

Thinking and writing positive thoughts

_____

_____

_____

Loving yourself

_____

_____

_____

DAY 213

I am grateful for the never-ending
supply of divine abundance in my life.

♡ ♡ ♡ ♡ ♡

Set your intentions for the day by...

Repeating the affirmation

_____

_____

_____

Thinking and writing positive thoughts

_____

_____

_____

Loving yourself

_____

_____

_____

DAY 214

I am gifted by divine abundance.
I am blessed and I am grateful.

♡   ♡   ♡   ♡   ♡

Set your intentions for the day by...

Repeating the affirmation

_____

_____

_____

Thinking and writing positive thoughts

_____

_____

_____

Loving yourself

_____

_____

_____

DAY 215

Divine abundance is my life. I am grateful
for the changes that it brings me.

♡ ♡ ♡ ♡ ♡

Set your intentions for the day by...

Repeating the affirmation

_____

_____

_____

Thinking and writing positive thoughts

_____

_____

_____

Loving yourself

_____

_____

_____

DAY 216

I know that each and every thought that I have creates the reality of divine abundance in my life and I am grateful.

♡ ♡ ♡ ♡ ♡

Set your intentions for the day by...

Repeating the affirmation

_____

_____

_____

Thinking and writing positive thoughts

_____

_____

_____

Loving yourself

_____

_____

_____

DAY 217

I am grateful for all that I have and for all that
I am. I am grateful for the gift of divine
abundance in my life.

♡　♡　♡　♡　♡

Set your intentions for the day by...

Repeating the affirmation

_____

_____

_____

Thinking and writing positive thoughts

_____

_____

_____

Loving yourself

_____

_____

_____

DAY 218

I am always open to receive divine
abundance in light, love, and in gratitude.

♡ ♡ ♡ ♡ ♡

Set your intentions for the day by...

Repeating the affirmation

_____

_____

_____

Thinking and writing positive thoughts

_____

_____

_____

Loving yourself

_____

_____

_____

DAY 219

There is more than enough divine abundance for everything and anything that I want. I give thanks and gratitude.

♡ ♡ ♡ ♡ ♡

Set your intentions for the day by...

Repeating the affirmation

_____

_____

_____

Thinking and writing positive thoughts

_____

_____

_____

Loving yourself

_____

_____

_____

DAY 220

Gratitude has created the space for divine abundance.
I am in awe for all that has been provided.

♡ ♡ ♡ ♡ ♡

Set your intentions for the day by...

Repeating the affirmation

_____

_____

_____

Thinking and writing positive thoughts

_____

_____

_____

Loving yourself

_____

_____

_____

DAY 221

I am worthy to receive the gift of divine abundance. I am grateful for these gifts.

♡ ♡ ♡ ♡ ♡

Set your intentions for the day by...

Repeating the affirmation

_____

_____

_____

Thinking and writing positive thoughts

_____

_____

_____

Loving yourself

_____

_____

_____

DAY 222

My thoughts, words, and deeds have created divine abundance in my life. I give thanks with gratitude.

♡ ♡ ♡ ♡ ♡

Set your intentions for the day by...

Repeating the affirmation

_____

_____

_____

Thinking and writing positive thoughts

_____

_____

_____

Loving yourself

_____

_____

_____

DAY 223

I am blessed knowing divine abundance
graces my life and I am grateful.

♡　　♡　　♡　　♡　　♡

Set your intentions for the day by...

Repeating the affirmation

_____

_____

_____

Thinking and writing positive thoughts

_____

_____

_____

Loving yourself

_____

_____

_____

DAY 224

I am grateful that divine abundance has opened
the doors for many blessings in my life.

♡ ♡ ♡ ♡ ♡

Set your intentions for the day by...

Repeating the affirmation

_____

_____

_____

Thinking and writing positive thoughts

_____

_____

_____

Loving yourself

_____

_____

_____

DAY 225

I know divine love and divine abundance
surround me. I am grateful for all that it brings.

♡ ♡ ♡ ♡ ♡

Set your intentions for the day by...

Repeating the affirmation

_____

_____

_____

Thinking and writing positive thoughts

_____

_____

_____

Loving yourself

_____

_____

_____

DAY 226

I am grateful that I am loved and that
divine abundance is all around me.

♡　♡　♡　♡　♡

Set your intentions for the day by...

Repeating the affirmation

_____

_____

_____

Thinking and writing positive thoughts

_____

_____

_____

Loving yourself

_____

_____

_____

DAY 227

I am grateful that divine abundance
is my natural state of being.

♡ ♡ ♡ ♡ ♡

Set your intentions for the day by...

Repeating the affirmation

_____

_____

_____

Thinking and writing positive thoughts

_____

_____

_____

Loving yourself

_____

_____

_____

DAY 228

I start each day with gratitude and appreciation for the divine abundance that flows to me.

♡　♡　♡　♡　♡

Set your intentions for the day by...

Repeating the affirmation

_____

_____

_____

Thinking and writing positive thoughts

_____

_____

_____

Loving yourself

_____

_____

_____

DAY 229

I gratefully accept all divine
abundance with love and grace.

♡　♡　♡　♡　♡

Set your intentions for the day by...

Repeating the affirmation

_____

_____

_____

Thinking and writing positive thoughts

_____

_____

_____

Loving yourself

_____

_____

_____

DAY 230

In gratitude, I expect the miracle of divine abundance to always be in my life.

♡ ♡ ♡ ♡ ♡

Set your intentions for the day by...

Repeating the affirmation

_____

_____

_____

Thinking and writing positive thoughts

_____

_____

_____

Loving yourself

_____

_____

_____

DAY 231

The doors of opportunity are fully open.
I gratefully accept these opportunities
and divine abundance into my life.

♡ ♡ ♡ ♡ ♡

Set your intentions for the day by...

Repeating the affirmation

_____

_____

_____

Thinking and writing positive thoughts

_____

_____

_____

Loving yourself

_____

_____

_____

DAY 232

The universe always supports me and provides for me in the form of divine abundance. I am grateful for such loving support.

♡   ♡   ♡   ♡   ♡

Set your intentions for the day by...

Repeating the affirmation

_____

_____

_____

Thinking and writing positive thoughts

_____

_____

_____

Loving yourself

_____

_____

_____

DAY 233

I am grateful for all that I have
through divine abundance.

♡　♡　♡　♡　♡

Set your intentions for the day by...

Repeating the affirmation

_____

_____

_____

Thinking and writing positive thoughts

_____

_____

_____

Loving yourself

_____

_____

_____

DAY 234

I acknowledge the divine presence in my life and I am grateful for the divine abundance that has been provided.

♡ ♡ ♡ ♡ ♡

Set your intentions for the day by...

Repeating the affirmation

_____

_____

_____

Thinking and writing positive thoughts

_____

_____

_____

Loving yourself

_____

_____

_____

DAY 235

I gratefully accept divine abundance into
my life and I know that I am blessed.

♡ ♡ ♡ ♡ ♡

Set your intentions for the day by...

Repeating the affirmation

_____

_____

_____

Thinking and writing positive thoughts

_____

_____

_____

Loving yourself

_____

_____

_____

DAY 236

Divine abundance is mine and I
gratefully accept it into my life.

♡　♡　♡　♡　♡

Set your intentions for the day by...

Repeating the affirmation

_____

_____

_____

Thinking and writing positive thoughts

_____

_____

_____

Loving yourself

_____

_____

_____

DAY 237

Divine abundance is reflected in
everything that I do and I am grateful.

♡ ♡ ♡ ♡ ♡

Set your intentions for the day by...

Repeating the affirmation

_____

_____

_____

Thinking and writing positive thoughts

_____

_____

_____

Loving yourself

_____

_____

_____

DAY 238

I gratefully attract divine abundance
with every thought that I have.

♡ ♡ ♡ ♡ ♡

Set your intentions for the day by...

Repeating the affirmation

_____

_____

_____

Thinking and writing positive thoughts

_____

_____

_____

Loving yourself

_____

_____

_____

DAY 239

I fully embrace the gift of divine abundance in my life. I gratefully give my thanks.

♡ ♡ ♡ ♡ ♡

Set your intentions for the day by...

Repeating the affirmation

_____

_____

_____

Thinking and writing positive thoughts

_____

_____

_____

Loving yourself

_____

_____

_____

DAY 240

I am grateful that divine abundance has
provided financial security and wealth.

♡ ♡ ♡ ♡ ♡

Set your intentions for the day by...

Repeating the affirmation

_____

_____

_____

Thinking and writing positive thoughts

_____

_____

_____

Loving yourself

_____

_____

_____

DAY 241

I am grateful that divine abundance
surrounds me wherever I go.

♡　♡　♡　♡　♡

Set your intentions for the day by...

Repeating the affirmation

_____

_____

_____

Thinking and writing positive thoughts

_____

_____

_____

Loving yourself

_____

_____

_____

DAY 242

Divine abundance is seen in all aspects of my life.
I am grateful for how blessed I am.

♡ ♡ ♡ ♡ ♡

Set your intentions for the day by...

Repeating the affirmation

_____

_____

_____

Thinking and writing positive thoughts

_____

_____

_____

Loving yourself

_____

_____

_____

DAY 243

I graciously and gratefully accept the
flow of divine abundance in my life.

♡　♡　♡　♡　♡

Set your intentions for the day by...

Repeating the affirmation

_____

_____

_____

Thinking and writing positive thoughts

_____

_____

_____

Loving yourself

_____

_____

_____

DAY 244

I love knowing that divine abundance
is my birthright and gratefully accept it.

♡　♡　♡　♡　♡

Set your intentions for the day by...

Repeating the affirmation

_____

_____

_____

Thinking and writing positive thoughts

_____

_____

_____

Loving yourself

_____

_____

_____

DAY 245

Prosperity, wealth, and divine abundance
always flow to me and I am grateful.

♡   ♡   ♡   ♡   ♡

Set your intentions for the day by...

Repeating the affirmation

_____

_____

_____

Thinking and writing positive thoughts

_____

_____

_____

Loving yourself

_____

_____

_____

DAY 246

The universe has blessed me with divine
abundance and I gratefully accept it into my life.

♡　♡　♡　♡　♡

Set your intentions for the day by...

Repeating the affirmation

_____

_____

_____

Thinking and writing positive thoughts

_____

_____

_____

Loving yourself

_____

_____

_____

DAY 247

Thank you, thank you, thank you! I love the flow of divine abundance into my life. I gratefully accept all it brings.

♡ ♡ ♡ ♡ ♡

Set your intentions for the day by...

Repeating the affirmation

_____

_____

_____

Thinking and writing positive thoughts

_____

_____

_____

Loving yourself

_____

_____

_____

DAY 248

I am grateful that I create and manifest divine
abundance in my life. I am blessed with
this miracle each and every day.

♡ ♡ ♡ ♡ ♡

Set your intentions for the day by...

Repeating the affirmation

_____

_____

_____

Thinking and writing positive thoughts

_____

_____

_____

Loving yourself

_____

_____

_____

DAY 249

Divine abundance is always in my life
I am grateful for all it brings to me.

♡ ♡ ♡ ♡ ♡

Set your intentions for the day by...

Repeating the affirmation

_____

_____

_____

Thinking and writing positive thoughts

_____

_____

_____

Loving yourself

_____

_____

_____

DAY 250

I am successful. I am prosperous. I am wealthy. Divine abundance graces my life. I am grateful for all of it.

♡ ♡ ♡ ♡ ♡

Set your intentions for the day by...

Repeating the affirmation

_____

_____

_____

Thinking and writing positive thoughts

_____

_____

_____

Loving yourself

_____

_____

_____

DAY 251

The divine protects me, provides for me, and has opened the doors so that divine abundance is always present in my life. I am eternally grateful.

♡ ♡ ♡ ♡ ♡

Set your intentions for the day by...

Repeating the affirmation

_____

_____

_____

Thinking and writing positive thoughts

_____

_____

_____

Loving yourself

_____

_____

_____

DAY 252

I joyfully and gratefully accept
divine abundance in my life.

♡ ♡ ♡ ♡ ♡

Set your intentions for the day by...

Repeating the affirmation

_____

_____

_____

Thinking and writing positive thoughts

_____

_____

_____

Loving yourself

_____

_____

_____

DAY 253

I am grateful for the divine abundance
that pours into my life in constant flow.

♡　♡　♡　♡　♡

Set your intentions for the day by...

Repeating the affirmation

_____

_____

_____

Thinking and writing positive thoughts

_____

_____

_____

Loving yourself

_____

_____

_____

DAY 254

Divine abundance provides an infinite source
of wealth in my life and I am grateful.

♡　♡　♡　♡　♡

Set your intentions for the day by...

Repeating the affirmation

_____

_____

_____

Thinking and writing positive thoughts

_____

_____

_____

Loving yourself

_____

_____

_____

DAY 255

Gratitude has allowed me to serve
through the riches of divine abundance.

♡ ♡ ♡ ♡ ♡

Set your intentions for the day by...

Repeating the affirmation

_____

_____

_____

Thinking and writing positive thoughts

_____

_____

_____

Loving yourself

_____

_____

_____

DAY 256

I am blessed and grateful for the divine
abundance that is always available to me.

♡ ♡ ♡ ♡ ♡

Set your intentions for the day by...

Repeating the affirmation

_____

_____

_____

Thinking and writing positive thoughts

_____

_____

_____

Loving yourself

_____

_____

_____

DAY 257

I love and I am grateful for the flow
of divine abundance in my life.

♡　♡　♡　♡　♡

Set your intentions for the day by...

Repeating the affirmation

_____

_____

_____

Thinking and writing positive thoughts

_____

_____

_____

Loving yourself

_____

_____

_____

DAY 258

Everyday, in every way, I am wealthier
through the blessing of divine abundance
in my life. I am grateful for all it brings.

♡ ♡ ♡ ♡ ♡

Set your intentions for the day by...

Repeating the affirmation

_____

_____

_____

Thinking and writing positive thoughts

_____

_____

_____

Loving yourself

_____

_____

_____

DAY 259

I am grateful for divine abundance in my life
and the opportunities that it brings.

♡　♡　♡　♡　♡

Set your intentions for the day by...

Repeating the affirmation

_____

_____

_____

Thinking and writing positive thoughts

_____

_____

_____

Loving yourself

_____

_____

_____

DAY 260

Divine abundance provides more than
enough financial security in all areas of my life.

♡   ♡   ♡   ♡   ♡

Set your intentions for the day by...

Repeating the affirmation

_____

_____

_____

Thinking and writing positive thoughts

_____

_____

_____

Loving yourself

_____

_____

_____

DAY 261

I am successful in manifesting divine abundance in my life. I am grateful for these blessings.

♡ ♡ ♡ ♡ ♡

Set your intentions for the day by...

Repeating the affirmation

_____

_____

_____

Thinking and writing positive thoughts

_____

_____

_____

Loving yourself

_____

_____

_____

DAY 262

I love and I am grateful for my success
in creating divine abundance in my life.

♡ ♡ ♡ ♡ ♡

Set your intentions for the day by...

Repeating the affirmation

_____

_____

_____

Thinking and writing positive thoughts

_____

_____

_____

Loving yourself

_____

_____

_____

DAY 263

Gratitude and thanks are my keys for
creating more divine abundance in my life.

♡   ♡   ♡   ♡   ♡

Set your intentions for the day by...

Repeating the affirmation

_____

_____

_____

Thinking and writing positive thoughts

_____

_____

_____

Loving yourself

_____

_____

_____

DAY 264

I am grateful that I am always in
the flow of divine abundance.

♡ ♡ ♡ ♡ ♡

Set your intentions for the day by...

Repeating the affirmation

_____

_____

_____

Thinking and writing positive thoughts

_____

_____

_____

Loving yourself

_____

_____

_____

DAY 265

I am grateful for the unlimited amounts of
prosperity, wealth, and divine abundance in my life.

♡ ♡ ♡ ♡ ♡

Set your intentions for the day by...

Repeating the affirmation

_____

_____

_____

Thinking and writing positive thoughts

_____

_____

_____

Loving yourself

_____

_____

_____

DAY 266

I draw to me infinite quantities of money and divine abundance in my life. I give thanks and show my gratitude in all that I do.

♡ ♡ ♡ ♡ ♡

Set your intentions for the day by...

Repeating the affirmation

_____

_____

_____

Thinking and writing positive thoughts

_____

_____

_____

Loving yourself

_____

_____

_____

DAY 267

I am grateful to have an unlimited flow of divine abundance so that all my needs and desires are met.

♡ ♡ ♡ ♡ ♡

Set your intentions for the day by...

Repeating the affirmation

_____

_____

_____

Thinking and writing positive thoughts

_____

_____

_____

Loving yourself

_____

_____

_____

DAY 268

I am grateful that divine abundance provides for all my needs and desires with the intention to use it for the highest and greatest good.

♡　♡　♡　♡　♡

Set your intentions for the day by...

Repeating the affirmation

_____

_____

_____

Thinking and writing positive thoughts

_____

_____

_____

Loving yourself

_____

_____

_____

DAY 269

Divine abundance flows to me through the
blessing of divine love and I am grateful.

♡ ♡ ♡ ♡ ♡

Set your intentions for the day by...

Repeating the affirmation

_____

_____

_____

Thinking and writing positive thoughts

_____

_____

_____

Loving yourself

_____

_____

_____

DAY 270

I am grateful to create a positive flow of divine abundance in all areas of my life.

♡　♡　♡　♡　♡

Set your intentions for the day by...

Repeating the affirmation

_____

_____

_____

Thinking and writing positive thoughts

_____

_____

_____

Loving yourself

_____

_____

_____

DAY 271

I am a magnet for success, wealth,
and divine abundance and I am grateful.

♡   ♡   ♡   ♡   ♡

Set your intentions for the day by...

Repeating the affirmation

_____

_____

_____

Thinking and writing positive thoughts

_____

_____

_____

Loving yourself

_____

_____

_____

DAY 272

Love, thanks, and gratitude manifest
divine abundance in my life.

♡ ♡ ♡ ♡ ♡

Set your intentions for the day by...

Repeating the affirmation

_____

_____

_____

Thinking and writing positive thoughts

_____

_____

_____

Loving yourself

_____

_____

_____

DAY 273

I am grateful that each moment increases
the flow of divine abundance in my life.

♡ ♡ ♡ ♡ ♡

Set your intentions for the day by...

Repeating the affirmation

_____

_____

_____

Thinking and writing positive thoughts

_____

_____

_____

Loving yourself

_____

_____

_____

DAY 274

I see the world in love and light. I am grateful
to manifest unlimited divine abundance in my life.

♡　♡　♡　♡　♡

Set your intentions for the day by...

Repeating the affirmation

_____

_____

_____

Thinking and writing positive thoughts

_____

_____

_____

Loving yourself

_____

_____

_____

DAY 275

I am grateful for the flow of inspiration and creativity in my life. The doors to receive divine abundance are open.

♡ ♡ ♡ ♡ ♡

Set your intentions for the day by...

Repeating the affirmation

_____

_____

_____

Thinking and writing positive thoughts

_____

_____

_____

Loving yourself

_____

_____

_____

DAY 276

I deserve the flow of divine abundance in my life. I give my thanks and gratitude daily.

♡ ♡ ♡ ♡ ♡

Set your intentions for the day by...

Repeating the affirmation

_____

_____

_____

Thinking and writing positive thoughts

_____

_____

_____

Loving yourself

_____

_____

_____

DAY 277

I am grateful that each day brings more and more
financial prosperity and divine abundance to my life.

♡ ♡ ♡ ♡ ♡

Set your intentions for the day by...

Repeating the affirmation

_____

_____

_____

Thinking and writing positive thoughts

_____

_____

_____

Loving yourself

_____

_____

_____

DAY 278

Wealth, prosperity, and divine abundance are my birthright. I accept these with gratitude.

♡　♡　♡　♡　♡

Set your intentions for the day by...

Repeating the affirmation

_____

_____

_____

Thinking and writing positive thoughts

_____

_____

_____

Loving yourself

_____

_____

_____

DAY 279

I have unlimited amounts of divine
abundance in my life and I am grateful.

♡　♡　♡　♡　♡

Set your intentions for the day by...

Repeating the affirmation

_____

_____

_____

Thinking and writing positive thoughts

_____

_____

_____

Loving yourself

_____

_____

_____

DAY 280

I am grateful and I expect the flow
of divine abundance in my life.

♡ ♡ ♡ ♡ ♡

Set your intentions for the day by...

Repeating the affirmation

_____

_____

_____

Thinking and writing positive thoughts

_____

_____

_____

Loving yourself

_____

_____

_____

DAY 281

I give my thanks and gratitude that I have financial freedom through the blessing of divine abundance.

♡ ♡ ♡ ♡ ♡

Set your intentions for the day by...

Repeating the affirmation

_____

_____

_____

Thinking and writing positive thoughts

_____

_____

_____

Loving yourself

_____

_____

_____

DAY 282

I am grateful for the guidance that is around me
and that divine abundance flows to me.

♡　♡　♡　♡　♡

Set your intentions for the day by...

Repeating the affirmation

_____

_____

_____

Thinking and writing positive thoughts

_____

_____

_____

Loving yourself

_____

_____

_____

DAY 283

Miracles are all around me and I am grateful for
the flow of divine abundance in my life.

♡　♡　♡　♡　♡

Set your intentions for the day by...

Repeating the affirmation

_____

_____

_____

Thinking and writing positive thoughts

_____

_____

_____

Loving yourself

_____

_____

_____

DAY 284

I accept, with gratitude, the blessing
of divine abundance into my life.

♡   ♡   ♡   ♡   ♡

Set your intentions for the day by...

Repeating the affirmation

_____

_____

_____

Thinking and writing positive thoughts

_____

_____

_____

Loving yourself

_____

_____

_____

DAY 285

I gratefully accept the energy of
divine abundance in my life.

♡ ♡ ♡ ♡ ♡

Set your intentions for the day by...

Repeating the affirmation

_____

_____

_____

Thinking and writing positive thoughts

_____

_____

_____

Loving yourself

_____

_____

_____

DAY 286

I live my life with love and gratitude for the creation and manifestation of divine abundance around me.

♡ ♡ ♡ ♡ ♡

Set your intentions for the day by...

Repeating the affirmation

_____

_____

_____

Thinking and writing positive thoughts

_____

_____

_____

Loving yourself

_____

_____

_____

DAY 287

I am focused with positive intent. I accept infinite amounts of divine abundance with gratitude.

♡　♡　♡　♡　♡

Set your intentions for the day by...

Repeating the affirmation

_____

_____

_____

Thinking and writing positive thoughts

_____

_____

_____

Loving yourself

_____

_____

_____

DAY 288

I give thanks and gratitude for the manifestation
of divine abundance in my life.

♡ ♡ ♡ ♡ ♡

Set your intentions for the day by...

Repeating the affirmation

_____

_____

_____

Thinking and writing positive thoughts

_____

_____

_____

Loving yourself

_____

_____

_____

DAY 289

Divine abundance and miracles are all around me and I am grateful to be so blessed.

♡ ♡ ♡ ♡ ♡

Set your intentions for the day by...

Repeating the affirmation

_____

_____

_____

Thinking and writing positive thoughts

_____

_____

_____

Loving yourself

_____

_____

_____

DAY 290

I am wealthy, successful, and prosperous
with unlimited divine abundance in my life.
I am grateful for the opportunities that it brings.

♡ ♡ ♡ ♡ ♡

Set your intentions for the day by...

Repeating the affirmation

_____

_____

_____

Thinking and writing positive thoughts

_____

_____

_____

Loving yourself

_____

_____

_____

DAY 291

I am serving through the grace of the divine and I am grateful for the divine abundance provided to me.

♡ ♡ ♡ ♡ ♡

Set your intentions for the day by...

Repeating the affirmation

_____

_____

_____

Thinking and writing positive thoughts

_____

_____

_____

Loving yourself

_____

_____

_____

DAY 292

I am blessed and grateful to be able to use the divine abundance in my life for the highest and greatest good.

♡ ♡ ♡ ♡ ♡

Set your intentions for the day by...

Repeating the affirmation

_____

_____

_____

Thinking and writing positive thoughts

_____

_____

_____

Loving yourself

_____

_____

_____

DAY 293

I manifest more and more divine abundance
each day with gratitude, love, light, and integrity.

♡ ♡ ♡ ♡ ♡

Set your intentions for the day by...

Repeating the affirmation

_____

_____

_____

Thinking and writing positive thoughts

_____

_____

_____

Loving yourself

_____

_____

_____

DAY 294

Money and divine abundance flow into
my life and I am grateful.

♡　♡　♡　♡　♡

Set your intentions for the day by...

Repeating the affirmation

_____

_____

_____

Thinking and writing positive thoughts

_____

_____

_____

Loving yourself

_____

_____

_____

DAY 295

I am grateful to follow the path of love and
light and accept divine abundance into my life.

♡ ♡ ♡ ♡ ♡

Set your intentions for the day by...

Repeating the affirmation

_____

_____

_____

Thinking and writing positive thoughts

_____

_____

_____

Loving yourself

_____

_____

_____

DAY 296

I am grateful that my every need is met through the manifestation of divine abundance my life.

♡   ♡   ♡   ♡   ♡

Set your intentions for the day by...

Repeating the affirmation

_____

_____

_____

Thinking and writing positive thoughts

_____

_____

_____

Loving yourself

_____

_____

_____

DAY 297

I honor the spiritual being that I am and I give thanks
with gratitude for divine abundance to fill my life.

♡   ♡   ♡   ♡   ♡

Set your intentions for the day by...

Repeating the affirmation

_____

_____

_____

Thinking and writing positive thoughts

_____

_____

_____

Loving yourself

_____

_____

_____

DAY 298

I manifest divine abundance for my highest and greatest good with joy, love, and gratitude.

♡ ♡ ♡ ♡ ♡

Set your intentions for the day by...

Repeating the affirmation

_____

_____

_____

Thinking and writing positive thoughts

_____

_____

_____

Loving yourself

_____

_____

_____

DAY 299

I am always grateful that I have more than enough through the flow of divine abundance in my life.

♡ ♡ ♡ ♡ ♡

Set your intentions for the day by...

Repeating the affirmation

_____

_____

_____

Thinking and writing positive thoughts

_____

_____

_____

Loving yourself

_____

_____

_____

DAY 300

I am grateful that everything I do increases the
flow of divine abundance in my life.

♡　♡　♡　♡　♡

Set your intentions for the day by...

Repeating the affirmation

_____

_____

_____

Thinking and writing positive thoughts

_____

_____

_____

Loving yourself

_____

_____

_____

DAY 301

I give thanks and gratitude that I am divinely
guided and blessed by divine abundance.

♡ ♡ ♡ ♡ ♡

Set your intentions for the day by...

Repeating the affirmation

_____

_____

_____

Thinking and writing positive thoughts

_____

_____

_____

Loving yourself

_____

_____

_____

DAY 302

I deserve divine abundance in my life
and I am grateful for all that it brings.

♡ ♡ ♡ ♡ ♡

Set your intentions for the day by...

Repeating the affirmation

_____

_____

_____

Thinking and writing positive thoughts

_____

_____

_____

Loving yourself

_____

_____

_____

DAY 303

I accept with love and gratitude infinite
amounts of divine abundance in my life.

♡ ♡ ♡ ♡ ♡

Set your intentions for the day by...

Repeating the affirmation

_____

_____

_____

Thinking and writing positive thoughts

_____

_____

_____

Loving yourself

_____

_____

_____

DAY 304

I am grateful that I am prosperous. Divine abundance flows easily and effortlessly into my life.

♡   ♡   ♡   ♡   ♡

Set your intentions for the day by...

Repeating the affirmation

_____

_____

_____

Thinking and writing positive thoughts

_____

_____

_____

Loving yourself

_____

_____

_____

DAY 305

I gratefully accept divine abundance into my life.

♡ ♡ ♡ ♡ ♡

Set your intentions for the day by...

Repeating the affirmation

_____

_____

_____

Thinking and writing positive thoughts

_____

_____

_____

Loving yourself

_____

_____

_____

DAY 306

Divine abundance blesses me. I give thanks and gratitude for all it brings to my life.

♡   ♡   ♡   ♡   ♡

Set your intentions for the day by...

Repeating the affirmation

_____

_____

_____

Thinking and writing positive thoughts

_____

_____

_____

Loving yourself

_____

_____

_____

DAY 307

I am grateful for the substantial flow of divine
abundance that comes to me now.

♡ ♡ ♡ ♡ ♡

Set your intentions for the day by...

Repeating the affirmation

_____

_____

_____

Thinking and writing positive thoughts

_____

_____

_____

Loving yourself

_____

_____

_____

DAY 308

I am grateful there is always more than enough
wealth and divine abundance for all.

♡　♡　♡　♡　♡

Set your intentions for the day by...

Repeating the affirmation

_____

_____

_____

Thinking and writing positive thoughts

_____

_____

_____

Loving yourself

_____

_____

_____

DAY 309

I am open and grateful for the constant
flow of divine abundance in my life.

♡　♡　♡　♡　♡

Set your intentions for the day by...

Repeating the affirmation

_____

_____

_____

Thinking and writing positive thoughts

_____

_____

_____

Loving yourself

_____

_____

_____

DAY 310

Through divine love, divine abundance
is in constant flow in my life. I am grateful.

♡   ♡   ♡   ♡   ♡

Set your intentions for the day by...

Repeating the affirmation

_____

_____

_____

Thinking and writing positive thoughts

_____

_____

_____

Loving yourself

_____

_____

_____

DAY 311

Divine love and abundance is a constant
force in my life and I am grateful.

♡　♡　♡　♡　♡

Set your intentions for the day by...

Repeating the affirmation

_____

_____

_____

Thinking and writing positive thoughts

_____

_____

_____

Loving yourself

_____

_____

_____

DAY 312

I am a magnet for divine abundance and
I am grateful for all that is created in my life.

♡ ♡ ♡ ♡ ♡

Set your intentions for the day by...

Repeating the affirmation

_____

_____

_____

Thinking and writing positive thoughts

_____

_____

_____

Loving yourself

_____

_____

_____

DAY 313

I am grounded and secure with the infinite amounts of divine abundance in my life. I am grateful for all it brings.

♡　♡　♡　♡　♡

Set your intentions for the day by...

Repeating the affirmation

_____

_____

_____

Thinking and writing positive thoughts

_____

_____

_____

Loving yourself

_____

_____

_____

DAY 314

I am grateful for the choice to live a
life of divine abundance.

♡ ♡ ♡ ♡ ♡

Set your intentions for the day by...

Repeating the affirmation

_____

_____

_____

Thinking and writing positive thoughts

_____

_____

_____

Loving yourself

_____

_____

_____

DAY 315

I appreciate and I am grateful for
divine abundance in my life.

♡　♡　♡　♡　♡

Set your intentions for the day by...

Repeating the affirmation

_____

_____

_____

Thinking and writing positive thoughts

_____

_____

_____

Loving yourself

_____

_____

_____

DAY 316

My heart is open with love and I gratefully
accept divine abundance into my life.

♡   ♡   ♡   ♡   ♡

Set your intentions for the day by...

Repeating the affirmation

_____

_____

_____

Thinking and writing positive thoughts

_____

_____

_____

Loving yourself

_____

_____

_____

DAY 317

I am grateful that my heart is open for
unlimited divine abundance to flow to me.

♡　♡　♡　♡　♡

Set your intentions for the day by...

Repeating the affirmation

_____

_____

_____

Thinking and writing positive thoughts

_____

_____

_____

Loving yourself

_____

_____

_____

DAY 318

I am secure, happy, and grateful for an infinite flow of divine abundance in my life.

♡　♡　♡　♡　♡

Set your intentions for the day by...

Repeating the affirmation

_____

_____

_____

Thinking and writing positive thoughts

_____

_____

_____

Loving yourself

_____

_____

_____

DAY 319

I create and manifest daily miracles in my life. I am grateful for the flow of divine abundance that is all around me.

♡ ♡ ♡ ♡ ♡

Set your intentions for the day by...

Repeating the affirmation

_____

_____

_____

Thinking and writing positive thoughts

_____

_____

_____

Loving yourself

_____

_____

_____

DAY 320

Thank you, thank you, thank you! Divine love
and gratitude has made it possible for
divine abundance to be present in my life.

♡ ♡ ♡ ♡ ♡

Set your intentions for the day by...

Repeating the affirmation

_____

_____

_____

Thinking and writing positive thoughts

_____

_____

_____

Loving yourself

_____

_____

_____

DAY 321

I am divinely guided in all that I do and I give
thanks and gratitude for the outward
manifestation of divine abundance in my life.

♡ ♡ ♡ ♡ ♡

Set your intentions for the day by...

Repeating the affirmation

_____

_____

_____

Thinking and writing positive thoughts

_____

_____

_____

Loving yourself

_____

_____

_____

DAY 322

I have an open invitation for success, prosperity,
and divine abundance to flow to me and I am grateful.

♡　♡　♡　♡　♡

Set your intentions for the day by...

Repeating the affirmation

_____

_____

_____

Thinking and writing positive thoughts

_____

_____

_____

Loving yourself

_____

_____

_____

DAY 323

I serve those around me with an open
heart and I am grateful for the manifestation
of divine abundance in our lives.

♡ ♡ ♡ ♡ ♡

Set your intentions for the day by...

Repeating the affirmation

_____

_____

_____

Thinking and writing positive thoughts

_____

_____

_____

Loving yourself

_____

_____

_____

DAY 324

I am grateful and thankful that I have the opportunity
to accept divine abundance in all areas of my life.

♡ ♡ ♡ ♡ ♡

Set your intentions for the day by...

Repeating the affirmation

_____

_____

_____

Thinking and writing positive thoughts

_____

_____

_____

Loving yourself

_____

_____

_____

DAY 325

I am grateful that divine abundance flows
to me, through me, and surrounds me.

♡　♡　♡　♡　♡

Set your intentions for the day by...

Repeating the affirmation

_____

_____

_____

Thinking and writing positive thoughts

_____

_____

_____

Loving yourself

_____

_____

_____

DAY 326

I create and manifest all good things in my life.
I am grateful for divine abundance.

♡ ♡ ♡ ♡ ♡

Set your intentions for the day by...

Repeating the affirmation

_____

_____

_____

Thinking and writing positive thoughts

_____

_____

_____

Loving yourself

_____

_____

_____

DAY 327

I experience joy in the creation of divine abundance in my life. I am grateful for unlimited success, wealth, and prosperity.

♡ ♡ ♡ ♡ ♡

Set your intentions for the day by...

Repeating the affirmation

_____

_____

_____

Thinking and writing positive thoughts

_____

_____

_____

Loving yourself

_____

_____

_____

DAY 328

I am grateful that the doorway to opportunity is open and that divine abundance flows through.

♡ ♡ ♡ ♡ ♡

Set your intentions for the day by...

Repeating the affirmation

_____

_____

_____

Thinking and writing positive thoughts

_____

_____

_____

Loving yourself

_____

_____

_____

DAY 329

My light extends outward to create divine abundance for myself. I hold the space for others to create as well. I am grateful.

♡ ♡ ♡ ♡ ♡

Set your intentions for the day by...

Repeating the affirmation

_____

_____

_____

Thinking and writing positive thoughts

_____

_____

_____

Loving yourself

_____

_____

_____

DAY 330

Thank you divine source of all there is. I gratefully accept the divine abundance that is offered to me.

♡ ♡ ♡ ♡ ♡

Set your intentions for the day by...

Repeating the affirmation

_____

_____

_____

Thinking and writing positive thoughts

_____

_____

_____

Loving yourself

_____

_____

_____

DAY 331

The light of the divine surrounds me and provides divine abundance for my every need and desire. I am grateful for the gifts provided.

♡ ♡ ♡ ♡ ♡

Set your intentions for the day by...

Repeating the affirmation

_____

_____

_____

Thinking and writing positive thoughts

_____

_____

_____

Loving yourself

_____

_____

_____

DAY 332

I am light, I am love, I am happiness, and I am joy.
I gratefully accept divine abundance into my life.

♡ ♡ ♡ ♡ ♡

Set your intentions for the day by...

Repeating the affirmation

_____

_____

_____

Thinking and writing positive thoughts

_____

_____

_____

Loving yourself

_____

_____

_____

DAY 333

I am grateful that divine abundance
provides financial freedom in my life.

♡　♡　♡　♡　♡

Set your intentions for the day by...

Repeating the affirmation

_____

_____

_____

Thinking and writing positive thoughts

_____

_____

_____

Loving yourself

_____

_____

_____

DAY 334

I allow divine abundance into my life
and I am grateful for all it brings.

♡ ♡ ♡ ♡ ♡

Set your intentions for the day by...

Repeating the affirmation

_____

_____

_____

Thinking and writing positive thoughts

_____

_____

_____

Loving yourself

_____

_____

_____

DAY 335

I am grateful that the light in me creates
unlimited divine abundance in my life.

♡   ♡   ♡   ♡   ♡

Set your intentions for the day by...

Repeating the affirmation

_____

_____

_____

Thinking and writing positive thoughts

_____

_____

_____

Loving yourself

_____

_____

_____

DAY 336

I am grateful, to love and trust, that divine
love will manifest divine abundance in my life.

♡　♡　♡　♡　♡

Set your intentions for the day by...

Repeating the affirmation

_____

_____

_____

Thinking and writing positive thoughts

_____

_____

_____

Loving yourself

_____

_____

_____

DAY 337

Gratitude has moved me to a space of
divine abundance and I am grateful.

♡　♡　♡　♡　♡

Set your intentions for the day by...

Repeating the affirmation

_____

_____

_____

Thinking and writing positive thoughts

_____

_____

_____

Loving yourself

_____

_____

_____

DAY 338

I always experience divine abundance
in my life with gratitude.

♡ ♡ ♡ ♡ ♡

Set your intentions for the day by...

Repeating the affirmation

_____

_____

_____

Thinking and writing positive thoughts

_____

_____

_____

Loving yourself

_____

_____

_____

DAY 339

I give my sincerest thanks and gratitude that divine abundance is always a part of my life.

♡　♡　♡　♡　♡

Set your intentions for the day by...

Repeating the affirmation

_____

_____

_____

Thinking and writing positive thoughts

_____

_____

_____

Loving yourself

_____

_____

_____

DAY 340

I am always in touch with the divine abundance
around me. I am grateful for my awareness.

♡   ♡   ♡   ♡   ♡

Set your intentions for the day by...

Repeating the affirmation

_____

_____

_____

Thinking and writing positive thoughts

_____

_____

_____

Loving yourself

_____

_____

_____

DAY 341

Thank you! Thank you! Thank you for divine abundance. I am grateful for all that is in my life.

♡　♡　♡　♡　♡

Set your intentions for the day by...

Repeating the affirmation

_____

_____

_____

Thinking and writing positive thoughts

_____

_____

_____

Loving yourself

_____

_____

_____

DAY 342

I am full of joy, happiness, and gratitude for
the manifestation of divine abundance in my life.

♡　♡　♡　♡　♡

Set your intentions for the day by...

Repeating the affirmation

_____

_____

_____

Thinking and writing positive thoughts

_____

_____

_____

Loving yourself

_____

_____

_____

DAY 343

The more I share my love with the world, the more I am blessed with divine abundance. I am grateful for all it has brought.

♡ ♡ ♡ ♡ ♡

Set your intentions for the day by...

Repeating the affirmation

_____

_____

_____

Thinking and writing positive thoughts

_____

_____

_____

Loving yourself

_____

_____

_____

DAY 344

Each day is an opportunity for me to manifest divine abundance through love and gratitude.

♡　♡　♡　♡　♡

Set your intentions for the day by...

Repeating the affirmation

_____

_____

_____

Thinking and writing positive thoughts

_____

_____

_____

Loving yourself

_____

_____

_____

DAY 345

I believe in gratitude. I believe in success.
I believe in prosperity. I believe in divine abundance.

♡ ♡ ♡ ♡ ♡

Set your intentions for the day by...

Repeating the affirmation

_____

_____

_____

Thinking and writing positive thoughts

_____

_____

_____

Loving yourself

_____

_____

_____

DAY 346

Divine light and love are all around me. It is
natural for the miracle of divine abundance in
my life. I am grateful for all that I have.

♡ ♡ ♡ ♡ ♡

Set your intentions for the day by...

Repeating the affirmation

_____

_____

_____

Thinking and writing positive thoughts

_____

_____

_____

Loving yourself

_____

_____

_____

DAY 347

I move forward through life manifesting
and creating divine abundance wherever I go.
I am grateful for how it has touched my life.

♡ ♡ ♡ ♡ ♡

Set your intentions for the day by...

Repeating the affirmation

_____

_____

_____

Thinking and writing positive thoughts

_____

_____

_____

Loving yourself

_____

_____

_____

DAY 348

Gratitude has unlocked the doors to divine abundance.
I accept all that is being provided.

♡ ♡ ♡ ♡ ♡

Set your intentions for the day by...

Repeating the affirmation

_____

_____

_____

Thinking and writing positive thoughts

_____

_____

_____

Loving yourself

_____

_____

_____

DAY 349

I live in a state of grace.
Miracles and divine abundance surround me.
I express my gratitude for all that is given.

♡　♡　♡　♡　♡

Set your intentions for the day by...

Repeating the affirmation

_____

_____

_____

Thinking and writing positive thoughts

_____

_____

_____

Loving yourself

_____

_____

_____

DAY 350

I am grateful for the opportunities provided to me and blessed for the divine abundance that flows to me.

♡ ♡ ♡ ♡ ♡

Set your intentions for the day by...

Repeating the affirmation

_____

_____

_____

Thinking and writing positive thoughts

_____

_____

_____

Loving yourself

_____

_____

_____

DAY 351

I am grateful that divine abundance is all around me.
I say thank you, thank you, and thank you!

♡ ♡ ♡ ♡ ♡

Set your intentions for the day by...

Repeating the affirmation

_____

_____

_____

Thinking and writing positive thoughts

_____

_____

_____

Loving yourself

_____

_____

_____

DAY 352

Divine abundance is my birthright. I am grateful
and graciously accept it into my life.

♡ ♡ ♡ ♡ ♡

Set your intentions for the day by...

Repeating the affirmation

_____

_____

_____

Thinking and writing positive thoughts

_____

_____

_____

Loving yourself

_____

_____

_____

DAY 353

Divine abundance comes to me naturally.
I am grateful for all that I have.

♡ ♡ ♡ ♡ ♡

Set your intentions for the day by...

Repeating the affirmation

_____

_____

_____

Thinking and writing positive thoughts

_____

_____

_____

Loving yourself

_____

_____

_____

DAY 354

Divine abundance surrounds me
and gratitude brings more.

♡　♡　♡　♡　♡

Set your intentions for the day by...

Repeating the affirmation

_____

_____

_____

Thinking and writing positive thoughts

_____

_____

_____

Loving yourself

_____

_____

_____

DAY 355

I am grateful to accept the energy of divine abundance into my life.

♡ ♡ ♡ ♡ ♡

Set your intentions for the day by...

Repeating the affirmation

_____

_____

_____

Thinking and writing positive thoughts

_____

_____

_____

Loving yourself

_____

_____

_____

DAY 356

My every need and desire is met through gratitude
and divine abundance for all that I have.

♡　♡　♡　♡　♡

Set your intentions for the day by...

Repeating the affirmation

_____

_____

_____

Thinking and writing positive thoughts

_____

_____

_____

Loving yourself

_____

_____

_____

DAY 357

All that I ever need has been provided through the flow of divine abundance. I am grateful for all it brings.

♡ ♡ ♡ ♡ ♡

Set your intentions for the day by...

Repeating the affirmation

_____

_____

_____

Thinking and writing positive thoughts

_____

_____

_____

Loving yourself

_____

_____

_____

DAY 358

I am grateful that I attract
divine abundance in my life.

♡ ♡ ♡ ♡ ♡

Set your intentions for the day by...

Repeating the affirmation

_____

_____

_____

Thinking and writing positive thoughts

_____

_____

_____

Loving yourself

_____

_____

_____

DAY 359

Love and light surrounds me. I am grateful
for the miracle of divine abundance in my life.

♡ ♡ ♡ ♡ ♡

Set your intentions for the day by...

Repeating the affirmation

_____

_____

_____

Thinking and writing positive thoughts

_____

_____

_____

Loving yourself

_____

_____

_____

DAY 360

The universe always provides for me. Divine abundance is all around me and I am grateful.

♡   ♡   ♡   ♡   ♡

Set your intentions for the day by...

Repeating the affirmation

_____

_____

_____

Thinking and writing positive thoughts

_____

_____

_____

Loving yourself

_____

_____

_____

DAY 361

Divine abundance flows to me with ease
and grace. I accept this in my life with gratitude.

♡ ♡ ♡ ♡ ♡

Set your intentions for the day by...

Repeating the affirmation

_____

_____

_____

Thinking and writing positive thoughts

_____

_____

_____

Loving yourself

_____

_____

_____

DAY 362

With gratitude, I accept the constant
flow of divine abundance in my life.

♡ ♡ ♡ ♡ ♡

Set your intentions for the day by...

Repeating the affirmation

_____

_____

_____

Thinking and writing positive thoughts

_____

_____

_____

Loving yourself

_____

_____

_____

DAY 363

Divine abundance is always present in my life.
I am grateful for the constant flow.

♡　♡　♡　♡　♡

Set your intentions for the day by...

Repeating the affirmation

_____

_____

_____

Thinking and writing positive thoughts

_____

_____

_____

Loving yourself

_____

_____

_____

DAY 364

I am embraced in light and love. I gratefully accept the divine abundance that flows to me.

♡ ♡ ♡ ♡ ♡

Set your intentions for the day by...

Repeating the affirmation

_____

_____

_____

Thinking and writing positive thoughts

_____

_____

_____

Loving yourself

_____

_____

_____

DAY 365

I am aligned with the divine and I accept divine abundance in love, with gratitude.

♡ ♡ ♡ ♡ ♡

Set your intentions for the day by...

Repeating the affirmation

_____

_____

_____

Thinking and writing positive thoughts

_____

_____

_____

Loving yourself

_____

_____

_____

About The Author

Lisa has diverse experience and a true desire to assist each client compassionately, ethically, and in a space of love. She uses various tools and modalities to prepare and assist the body, mind, and spirit in beginning the healing process. Lisa will guide you through the journey of healing and toward awakening your own powers of self-awareness, self-healing, and well-being.

For a full list of products and services offered by Lisa, please visit

www.earthandbeyondtherapies.com

- Crystal Healing/Chakra Balancing
- Psychic/Intuitive readings
- Reiki Sessions and Training
- Spiritual Empowerment Coaching
- Spiritual Response Therapy (SRT)
- Young Living essential oils
- Crystals
- Oracle Cards
- And more

Earth And Beyond Crystal Therapies, LLC dba
Earth And Beyond Healing Therapies

32564809R00210

Made in the USA
Middletown, DE
08 June 2016